REFLECTIVE THEOLOGY

Philosophical Orientations in Religion

BY THOMAS N. MUNSON

New Haven and London | *Yale University Press*

1968

Library of Congress catalog card number: 68–27763

Designed by John O. C. McCrillis,
set in Baskerville type,
and printed in the United States of America by
The Carl Purington Rollins Printing-Office of
the Yale University Press, New Haven, Connecticut.
Distributed in Great Britain, Europe, Asia, and
Africa by Yale University Press Ltd., London; in
Canada by McGill University Press, Montreal; and
in Latin America by Centro Interamericano de Libros
Académicos, Mexico City.

REFLECTIVE THEOLOGY

*To Calvert House friends and
DePaul University colleagues*

PREFACE

As a nontheologian, I find it refreshing to read a religious book without being confronted on every other page with reflections or comments on *Honest to God, The Secular City,* or the God-is-dead theology; in short to discover a book that departs from the provincialism of the latest crisis, fashion, or cliché of Western religious language and traditions. This does not mean that the author is not passionately involved in many contemporary debates. On the contrary, he carefully analyzes, for instance, the later Wittgenstein and the latest Sartre—the Sartre of *Critique de la Raison Dialectique* and *Les Mots*—and he is aware of the growing influence of Lévi-Strauss' theories and method. But so far as I can judge the novelty of Thomas Munson's theological enterprise does not lie in his dialogue with some of the most powerful, belligerent and popular expressions of modern Western atheism (which, as Jacques Maritain candidly pointed out, sometimes reflect only a religious illiteracy). The significant novelty of this book consists in its opening new perspectives for a future theological discourse.

Like Paul Ricoeur, Thomas Munson has understood the importance of meditating and analyzing philosophically some religious beliefs and ideas of the "primitives" and Asiatic peoples. In other words, he does not restrict the "modernity" with which he wants to establish a dialogue to the most famous of the Western philosophical and artistic contemporary movements. He realizes that one of the elements of this "modernity" is constituted precisely by the discovery and understanding of the nonchristian religions— "primitive" as well as "exotic." One can say that this author arrives at the same conclusions as did Paul Tillich at the end of his life, namely, that a meaningful reformulation of Christian theology ought not only to confront the technological, desacralized societies of the West but also to establish a dialogue with the religions that originated and unfolded outside the Judaeo-Christian traditions. In short the theologian as well as the philosopher must utilize the works of the historians and the phenomenologists of religions and integrate their hermeneutics into his own systematic construction.

It is encouraging to discover in such a book as this interpretations of archaic myths and references to many outstanding orientalists and anthropologists. It is only a beginning and, I may add, a rather modest one. For the moment the few authors who have tried philosophically to discuss archaic and exotic religious experiences, symbols, and mythologies are still timid. One might imagine what the impetus of Ricoeur's brilliant exegesis could be if, instead of restricting his readings to the ancient Near East, he had discovered the amazingly rich spiritual worlds of Asia—and especially if he had not gathered his information about and borrowed the understanding of the "primitives" from Lévi-Strauss' *Structural Anthropology* and *The Savage Mind*. (One is unfortunately reminded of the times when the psychologists and philosophers collected their "facts and interpretations" from the books of Lévi-Bruhl, despite the fact that no ethnologist or responsible historian of religions accepted Lévi-Bruhl's hypothesis of "pre-logical mentality" and "mystical participation" of the primitives.)

Thomas Munson has realized the importance for the theologian and the philosopher of the fact that it was the experience of the sacred—an encounter with a transhuman reality—which gave birth to the idea that something really exists: that there are absolute values capable of guiding man and giving a meaning to human existence. It is, then, through the experience of the sacred that the ideas of reality, truth, and significance first dawned, to be later elaborated and systematized by metaphysical speculations. The apodictic value of myth is periodically reconfirmed by rituals. Recollection and reenactment of the primordial event help "primitive" men to distinguish and hold to the Real. By virtue of the continual repetition of a paradigmatic act, something shows itself to be fixed and enduring in the universal flux. This periodic reiteration of what was done *in illo tempore* makes it inescapably certain that something exists absolutely. This "something" is "sacred"—transhuman and transmundane—but it is accessible to human experience. Reality unveils itself and admits of being constructed from a transcendental level, but this transcendence can be ritually experienced and finally becomes an integral part of human life.

It is also of great importance for the theologian and the philosopher that, on the most archaic levels of culture, living as a human being is in itself a religious act. For on the one hand, alimentation, sexual life, and work have a sacramental value; and on the other hand, men assume the responsibility of preserving the "World" as it was made by the supernatural beings, periodically regenerating their world through rituals.

The last two generations of theologians and philosophers were almost exclusively preoccupied with the problems raised by the correct understanding of history and of the historicity of human existence. Few among these authors realized, however, that the "lesson of history" was already assimilated by Western consciousness, and that almost everything which could be written in the near future on these problems risked being epigonic and obsolete (as is already the case with a great part of the most recent theological literature). For myself, a nontheologian, it is still an enigma why only a few theologians and philosophers of religion

have understood the deep meaning of Teilhard de Chardin's
popular success. For it is evident that the main reason for
this unheard-of popularity lies in Teilhard's daring revaluation of the sacredness of life and matter. I do not intend
to discuss the validity of Teilhard's approach; and of course
I do not suggest that theologians and philosophers of religion ought to accept Teilhard's orientation and follow
his method. But it is significant that the rediscovery of life's
sacredness—which explains Teilhard's popularity among
laymen—parallels the sympathetic reassessment of the different types of "cosmic religion" that have captivated our
attention as a result of the hermeneutical work of historians
and phenomenologists of religion.

One need hardly add that there is no question of pro-
mulgating a new religious syncretism or of encouraging
new types of "paganism." But by understanding that for a
great part of the world, living as a human being is in itself
a religious act, a new, more profound and more generous
comprehension of the non-Judaeo-Christian world becomes
possible. In other words, a really "modern" systematic theology or philosophy of religion will have to take into consideration the totality of religious traditions, and not only
the monotheistic ones.

This is more easily said than done, for the Sacred is not
immediately recognizable in archaic and exotic religions;
at least not for those unfamiliar with the history of religions.
It was only recently that the religious dimensions of modern
literature and plastic arts and the religious presuppositions
of social and political movements were recognized; as a matter of fact they became evident as a result of the creative
analysis of some great theologians of culture. Similarly, only
through the hermeneutical work of historians and phenomenologists of religion will the omnipresence of the Sacred
become evident: the religious meaning and function of apparently secular images and symbols, of oral literatures and

plastic arts, of manual and intellectual work, and of social behavior and political ideologies of that immense world which opens beyond the frontiers of the Western *Oikumene.*

MIRCEA ELIADE

University of Chicago
May 1968

ACKNOWLEDGMENT

I wish to thank the Oxford University Press for permission to make use of selections from R. C. Zaehner's *Hinduism* (1962), and Routledge & Kegan Paul, Ltd., and The Humanities Press, Inc., for allowing citations from *Hegel's Lectures on the Philosophy of Religion*, 3 volumes edited and translated by Rev. E. B. Spiers and J. Burdon Sanderson. I am especially indebted to the Society for Religion in Higher Education for a cross-disciplinary fellowship during the academic year, 1965–66, and to the Rockefeller Foundation, whose grant in Hegelian studies made possible the leisure during which some of the reflections on Hegel matured. Were it not for these foundations I would not have been able to enjoy the courteous reception of Dean Jerald C. Brauer and the faculty of the University of Chicago Divinity School.

Throughout this book are traces of profitable discussions with students and faculty of Chicago's History of Religions department, particularly with Mircea Eliade and Charles Long. Everywhere the influence of Eliade's reflection will be apparent; hopefully the touch of his kindness will not be missed. Less evident to all but the author is the impact of hours of dialogue with Charles Long, whose open mind, agonizing doubts, and friendly probing are a fillip to enterprising scholarship. Finally, special thanks are due to my good friends and promoters: John Wild, Dr. Howard Schomer, and Father John McKenzie, S.J.

Thomas N. Munson

Chicago
1968

CONTENTS

ONE. PHILOSOPHY, THEOLOGY, AND RELIGION

Everyone who believes, thinks; for by believing he thinks, and by thinking he believes.

AUGUSTINE, *On the Predestination of Saints*

There are times when we read Saint Augustine with undisguised nostalgia. He must have won the battle over himself and brought his heart to peace because his writings betray a confident wholeness, a total, unified vision of man and his world. He announced the calm after the Pelagian storm and ushered the West into an era of relative tranquility that lasted until the time of Abelard and the recovery of the complete Aristotelian corpus in the twelfth century. During the high Middle Ages there were fresh attempts to establish on another basis a similar harmony of nature and grace, of reason and faith, of philosophy and theology. These were, at best, ephemeral triumphs of spirit, destined to crack by their very precariousness as syntheses. Once theology had been designated as systematized faith, as an intellectual construction aimed at understanding the revealed Word through the application of accepted philosophical categories, and philosophy had been assigned the presumably well-staked-out province of natural reason, it is obvious that the fate of Augustine's maxim, "Unless you believe, you will not understand," was sealed. Thanks to the developments of modern philosophy, this dictum was metamorphosed from a heuristic principle into a conundrum; owing to the linguistic bent of many contemporary philosophers, it is now a classic example of a meaningless statement.

In any case we would adjust with difficulty to Augustine's tranquil air. We can neither ignore the centuries of adaptations that make any present-day project of harmonizing philosophy, theology, and religion remotely analogous to his, nor can we expect to enter into a fruitful dialogue with specialists innocent of their critical internal problems, which have naturally grown in the course of the "information explosion." Moreover, at a time when many philosophers are convinced that description must replace explanation as the aim of philosophy, when Western theologians are required to cope with a "religionless" Christianity, and when investigators of religion—historians, anthropologists, sociologists, and the like—cannot agree on what constitutes a "religious fact," is not the suggestion of a unified view definitely premature?

Strange as it may sound, the renewed interest in the philosophy of religion would appear to indicate that this area may offer some hope for repaired communications. Why? Primarily because, amid all the academic revaluations that reflect our self-preoccupied society, the self-questionings of philosophers have been among the most anxious. Fortunately, although often undertaken in the sectarian spirit of justifying philosophical pursuits, these meditations have been in effect a courageous appraisal of the methods, the language, the evidence, and the presuppositions of all of our intellectual disciplines. In other words philosophy has recovered its critical function. It points proudly to its Socratic, Stoic, Peripatetic heritage, and proclaims itself less a system than a discipline, less a doctrine than a technique of reflection. The result, whatever one may say for the pretension, speaks for itself: a healing of some of the old interdisciplinary wounds, for philosophers are back in dialogue with theologians, scientists, artists, and historians.

This undeniable blessing has its inevitable drawback. Critics of the reflective notion of philosophy urge, not without reason, that with this concept the death of philosophy, like the death of God, has been announced. Philosophy must give way to a motley crew of philosophies—of history, of science, of law, of mathematics, and so forth. Besides, with this loss of independent status, the philosopher must surrender his claim to any special competence. Who, in this age of specialiaztion, is capable of criticizing intelligently, especially if an informed judgment requires that one be abreast of the latest findings of psychologists, linguists, and sociologists? For not only have ethnologists and anthropologists made significant contributions to religion—which the philosopher cannot ignore—but so have the proliferating numbers of scholars whose specialties we in the West usually group together as "theology": Scripture, patristics, Church history, dogmatics, and liturgics.

The seriousness of this charge cannot be dismissed offhand by noting that other disciplines face the same basic problem, even though it may be true that the philosopher of religion encounters merely an intensified form of the difficulty that besets, for instance, today's medical doctor. For when it is asserted that philosophy is a reflective technique, one wishes to emphasize that the philosophical aspect of any discipline consists in asking questions that ferret out the grounds or commitments of that discipline. Thus the physicist becomes a philosopher of science when his questions make him aware of the specificity of his enterprise: What constitutes his data? How does he test the validity of his research against other outlooks? Within a larger purview: Why should anyone ask this particular question? Does the fact that he asked it tell him anything about himself, his world? Ultimately these questions about our commitments are important because they reveal presuppositions about truth.

It is evident, then, that to situate philosophy in the "element" of reflection (to borrow Hegel's nebulous term) does not mean that the philosopher himself lacks position. No one, after all, can interrogate without direction. For the contemporary technical philosopher this direction has come in large measure from "the past," since one normally fixes his stance by entering into a dialogue with the great philosophers in order to master what they have to teach and to become sensitive to the limitations of their horizons. Yet even this stance is not fixed absolutely. Like ground, it can be firm yet from our standpoint shifting. New discoveries may require plottings in different areas, and critical assessment may exact deeper digging and more solid foundations. By stressing reflection, therefore, we are refining our understanding of position. We see, in fact, how paradoxically we stand, for a commitment is a position that we hold to be true, yet it is precisely the commitment that allows us to see this position as true.

When we look at the standard works on the philosophy of religion, we are likely to be astonished at how different their perspective can be from that offered by an emphatically reflective approach. Most of our anthologies repeat the traditional arguments and systems—of Anselm, Aquinas, Descartes, Kant, and so on—or present versions of these whose novelty consists mainly in the garniture of critical precisions or a reheating in linguistic sauce. It is a menu prepared by philosophers for philosophers: palatable to those who like this sort of fare but almost totally devoid of theological substance. Indeed, when Reason is thought to be a kind of spiritual lighthouse or disengaged faculty, the differences between the Leibnizian, Spinozistic, Humean, and Kantian discussions of God and our own are blotted out in its blinding light. If nothing else, the traditional philosophy of religion possessed the strength of simplicity. Whatever the variables, God and Reason remained the constants.

We can better appreciate the reaction of Karl Barth and many Protestant theologians (an impressionistic generalization, since the "older" theologians did not share their feelings about philosophical proofs for God, and today the pendulum seems to be swinging back again) to this "natural theology" when we understand that the philosophical discussion of immanence and transcendence was redolent of reductionism. Feuerbach, as we know, shrewdly discerned this and publicized the loss of one of the constants: theology had become anthropology. It was Nietzsche who later, with a clairvoyance deemed madness during his own lifetime, carried this death of God to its logical conclusion, the death of the Judaeo-Christian concept of man that had unwittingly survived as a guide and inspiration of Western thought. This message he delivered as a program for revaluating all values. Shocking as it was, he merely proclaimed openly what Descartes' philosophy asserted implicitly; for if the essence of man is "mind," then man as we know him is dead—and so, of course, is God.

By showing in this way the relationship between our concepts of God and man, Nietzsche contributed substantially to the revision of philosophy that has necessitated new ground rules for the philosophy of religion. If we are not disembodied minds, then more account must be taken of our incarnation. Thus, when Merleau-Ponty remarked that it is no longer fashionable to "prove God" after the example of Saint Thomas, Saint Anselm, and Descartes,[1] he was not rejecting the possibility of such arguments but emphasizing their apologetic limitations. Constructed for certain *milieux,* they no longer appeal. We find them curiously abstract, shaped by theological needs that are alien to us, and for the most part couched in a specialized vocabulary that to our ears often sounds odd. In a striking way they bring home to us the sense of our preoccupation with philosophy as a reflection: that we are concerned with the whole man as one who, because of his incarnation, occupies a definite place in history.

The apparently idiosyncratic composition of the chap-

1. *In Praise of Philosophy,* Eng. trans. John Wild and James Edie (Evanston, Northwestern University Press, 1963), p. 42.

ters of this book, in which the preliminary hermeneutical and critical problems of Chapters 2, 3, and 4 have been introduced in order to set the stage for a basic phenomenology of "the data," should be regarded as consequent upon this historical viewpoint. Obviously, the data of the philosophy of religion is merely that which is given to us, just as its "phenomena" are what manifest themselves to us and its problems woven from materials that appear significant to us. But our interests are formed by both present circumstances and past discussions, and the tools we have at hand for dealing with religious issues have been designed and collected mostly by our forebears. The reflection, then, that we shall undertake in this book can forcibly convince us that "raw data" forever remains a noble epistemological ideal. In cold fact, however, the reversion to previous approaches can highlight the philosophical and theological presuppositions that dictated them so that we become conscious of our own individual and group prejudices. A look back can reveal the areas that have been overworked and those that lie fallow; and although a return can be confusing because we see more clearly the complexity of a deceptively simple situation, still, we usually profit from it because we detect patterns—the recurring forms of problems which speak volumes about mankind. In every reflection we turn back upon ourselves (the historical beings *par excellence*), and so exhibit the truth of our position in the world. Were it not for reflection, the question of the truth of our implicit commitments would never be raised.

The point that we are making about the historicity of our reflection is often made more simply: we reflect as men, not as minds. Thinking is a matter of bringing a whole *Weltanschauung* to bear upon a topic. In the contemporary jargon we refer to this as existential thought, intending thereby to distinguish it from the peculiarly aseptic or bloodless type of categorizing commonly associated with school philosophy. Among the nonphilosophical, this latter is generally regarded as bordering on the esoteric. It resembles a contagious disease, something that one philosopher catches from another and transmits thereafter to his students.

The contemporary philosopher of religion who envisages his task reflectively thus finds himself in a dialogue with men committed to religion—in most cases defined as the dealings of a supernatural god with his creatures. As a philosopher, he probably will be interested in learning from the historians of religions to what extent it is proper to talk in universal terms about "the religious phenomenon" and in uncovering the available material for the construction of an authentic (Husserlian) phenomenology. What, he asks, are the fundamental religious structures of human consciousness? Having thus informed himself, he is then ready to engage the professional theologian in order to check out the consistency of a chosen intellectual scheme and to test its flexibility both as an heuristic instrument and as a satisfactory, up-to-date way of ordering things.

Conversely, a number of popular theologians have adopted philosophical mentors who allegedly speak more meaningfully to contemporary man. A welcome crossing of the abyss that has divided us since the days of the Enlightenment! But they have raised a number of serious difficulties for the professional philosopher: problems mainly connected with the application of principles and the commitments involved in accepting philosophical premises. Aside from the calculated temerity of identifying *the* contemporary mentality, does every contemporary viewpoint offer the materials for a viable theology? Bishop Robinson, for instance, seems mired in Humean empiricism, and so does Paul Van Buren because of his interpretation of Wittgenstein and selected linguistic analysts. Rudolf Bultmann finds the "early" Heidegger congenial but is strangely silent about the (logically consistent?) "later." Thomas Altizer stands, it would appear, upon the shoulders of Nietzsche,

whence he has glimpsed a vision of a dialectical or process
theology—one that unquestionably would make Hegel fear
for the future of dialectic. Harvey Cox has cited with ap-
proval the anti-metaphysical statements of Cornelis Van
Peursen, not merely because it is "identifying" to demonstrate against the "out" cause, but because "The Biblical
message is something quite different from . . . a doctrine of
the highest Being."[2]

It is indeed incontestable that a tribal culture and
nomadic existence are scarcely conducive to reflective or
speculative thought. But does not Van Peursen's apparently
obvious statement raise some critical doubts about the
Scriptures as historical documents? Since the biblical
exegetes have made us sensitive to the cultural relativity of
Hebraic and Greek formulations, in what sense can one
refer to a presumably crystal-clear biblical message? Are
we not guilty of disregarding or misunderstanding the historicity of man if we accept first-century cultural imagery
as perennial, while branding Neoplatonic and medieval patterns of intelligibility episodic? Moreover, does not this
statement suggest that metaphysics is a univocal concept
(and thus an easier target for polemicists), whereas one
might reasonably propose, without being especially con-
ciliatory, that all reflection, whether Aristotelian, Thom-
istic, Kantian, Hegelian, Whiteheadian, Russellian, or
Wittgensteinian, be labeled metaphysical? One detects in
Cox's anti-metaphysical, sociological orientation an impetus
from Auguste Comte, which naturally puzzles the philosopher. How respectable can a theological perspective be if
theology is actually the resort of the unregenerate, primitive mind?

Because our existential religious situation is complicated
by these philosophico–theological entanglements, we may

2. *The Secular City* (New York, Macmillan, 1965), p. 248, citing "Man
and Reality—The History of Human Thought," *The Student World*, 56
(1963), 20.

succeed in limning the contemporary issues more sharply by adopting a somewhat historical and person-centered approach. We do not intend in this work—this is the sense of the qualification somewhat—to discuss Saint Anselm within the confines of his immediate historical context, nor to dissect further his ontological argument with a view to exposing some new aspect of it. What we propose, rather, is an exercise in the history of ideas: a presentation more concerned with trends or movements of thought than precise temporal accuracy. Throughout, an exposition and interpretation of problems will therefore be aimed at helping us to face certain contemporary issues with a sense of their history. And how can we better understand a problem's provenance and subsequent evolution than by focusing upon the individuals whose names keep popping up in contemporary literature as having set it upon its course? It would be foolish, no doubt, to believe that Saint Anselm, when he began his proof in the Augustinian tradition of a prayer for light, was worried about our difficulty over a starting-point that owes much to Karl Barth. No, the genius of the Saint, which accounts for the enduring vitality of his thought, was that he reflected within a context in a way that has transcended the limitations of his context. Yet it is also true that, because he was a human, he either did not see all of the ramifications of his thought or experienced insights which were limited by his resources for working them.

All the thinkers chosen for consideration in this book cut similar figures. Descartes, in the concentrated religious focus in which we shall observe him, has thrown open to us the problem of a subjective hermeneutic; Hume, the intricacies and/or inadequacies of an objective hermeneutic; Hegel, the paradox of human thought in its dependence upon imagination; Wittgenstein, the tortured question of the meaning of 'God'; Eliade, the propriety of talking about religion in the midst of religions and of constructing a

meaningful phenomenology of religion; Sartre, the anxiety
of committing ourselves to any determinate point of view.
This book has been written in the belief that a personal
encounter with these men, even in a restricted way, can
prove to be for us a bona fide self-revelation. They help us
to formulate our questions and to be articulate about the
malaise that religious thinkers suggest as the cause of contemporary man's psychosis.

In another way will it appear that this book is person-
centered. It will reveal all too clearly the author's personal
interests and limited competence. But it will have served
its purpose if some of the issues are clarified, even though
its character as a reflection may make heavy demands upon
the nonspecialist reader, and if it contributes to furthering
a dialogue that is crucial to the fate of speculative theology.
Since it is improbable that anyone at this time commands
all the resources—historical, anthropological, sociological,
psychological, philosophical, and theological—necessary to
present religion in a broadly challenging intellectual manner, we must rely upon these personal encounters which,
after all, have always been the stimulus and sine qua non
of any religious experience.

TWO. THE PROBLEM OF A STARTING-POINT

Truly there is a god, although the fool has
said in his heart: there is no God.

SAINT ANSELM, *Proslogion*, CHAPTER II

It is generally recognized that the first step of the philosopher's journey is the critical one. Halting or buoyant, that
initial stride predetermines the main course of his investigation. Not that he has suddenly cut himself off from new
discoveries, or that all of his decisions have been made so
irrevocably that reconsiderations are unlikely. Such a blind
determinism extinguishes intellectual curiosity, the ani-
mating spirit of philosophy. But in any investigation a definitely "scientific" attitude has been assumed toward the
world: that it is in some fashion intelligible, capable of
responding to questions, and worth the time and trouble
of patient inquiry.

It has also been pointed out—and philosophers today
are not loathe to admit it—that a great deal more is assumed
at the outset than this minimal attitude. How, for example,
one formulates his philosophic enterprise depends upon a
complex network of presuppositions: the beliefs, as Peirce
designated them, that one betrays, as opposed to those he
parades. To begin with, the philosopher is ordinarily required to define his discipline. Yet even a superficial ac-
quaintance with the history of philosophy reveals that the
use of the word "philosophy" has evolved over the centuries. Most creative philosophers have supplied definitions
adapted to their principal interests. A case in point is our
suggestion that philosophy is essentially a reflective or critical activity. Even though this formulation may be accepted

as an accurate description, it can be assailed on the grounds that it eviscerates philosophy of all content. Can we pretend to science when our object is unspecified? And if philosophy is merely a technique of question-asking, it has to be thought of as "form" without "matter." In theory there is no limit to the further questions one can ask, and in practice the data or objects attracting our attention are too numerous and diverse to permit functional classification. Philosophy, therefore, in this understanding appears to have lost its scientific character.

The contemporary philosophers who have welcomed Wittgenstein's suggestion that the usual philosophical answers provoke more difficulties than they resolve view this anomaly as a sufficient reason for disqualifying philosophy as a science. Although they are wary of setting limits to philosophic activity and refuse on this account to specify an object that would structure their questions, they are principally dissatisfied with the traditional reply that philosophy is adequately distinguished as a science because its object is "Being." Here, then, is a clear illustration of how a definition has remarkable affinities to a slogan: it expresses a reactionary philosophical position.

One hesitates today in our anti-metaphysical climate of opinion to call attention to the obvious: that the description of philosophy as a critical activity implies certain ontological claims. Most clearly it entails a stand on the "critical problem": the interminable conflict over idealism and realism, subject and object, mind and world. To a certain type of realist, the insistence on philosophy as an activity is a subjectivist proposal: a suggestion that the unifying principles of criticism are simply the basic structures of the criticizing Ego. Since much of the traditional philosophy of religion has revolved about this point, whether religion, that is, is to be understood as a subjective formulation (or "emotion") or a knowledge of "objective fact," we shall have to uncover the premises at work shaping these descriptions and explore their consequences. For the present, it may suffice to note what a phenomenology of philosophy makes clear. From pre-Socratic times, philosophers have been interested in understanding or explaining everyday life. Simply speaking, they have been interested in thought and its expression in language and conduct, that is, in disclosing those presumed universally valid principles which "ground" the world and render its events intelligible.

In the course of its long history, different fashions of thought have been *à la mode,* sometimes logical, at other times metaphysical or empirical. But whatever the vogue, it has been emphasized that the nature of thought is systematic. Philosophers, for example, who have wished to impugn metaphysical thought have accused it of apriorism and parodied it as pure conceptualism, that is, as the construction of grandiose ideal schemes with little or no reference to the real world of empirical fact. No doubt this criticism has occasionally been warranted. Yet it cannot be leveled indiscriminately, and certainly not with an anti-systematic bias that suggests that the critic is free from presuppositions and a reasoned point of view. Thus in our days there would probably be considerably less antipathy to Hegel's work if greater attention were directed to his notion of *Aufhebung,* that thought is a process of relating. Anyone who thinks or theorizes unifies, and therefore his reasoning progresses within a context of relations, an "Absolute." Hegel tried to convey the dynamism of thought in his baffling terminology: "comprehension" *(Begreifen),* for example, and its related "con-cept" *(Begriff)* stress the activity of *taking together.* It is true that today we can do without many of Hegel's applications and bizarre interests. But his reflections on human knowledge as a logic or science of the *logos* are indispensable for appreciating the task of the contemporary philosopher of religion.

If we fit the self-questionings of contemporary philosophers into the movement of thought inaugurated by Hegel,

the inclination to offer a diagnosis of a mild or acute obsession symptomatic of radical insecurity will be recognized as
a failure to identify the signs of a meticulous search for a
philosophy of philosophy. Hegel's work can be interpreted
as sounding the death-knell of Cartesian rationalism and
Humean empiricism. Reason—and this is the import of his
phenomenology of the human spirit and his historical orientation—does not operate merely in the mathematical
hypothetico-deductive pattern or solely within the confines
of immediate empirical data. It is above all an activity of
harmonizing, so that "the reasonable" is circumscribed by
both the individual and social forces shaping what we
simply, yet ambiguously, denominate "experience." The
major problem, then, confronting the philosopher of religion is summed up in the question: "Why is religion—or
why has it been—absent from man's experience and its
articulation?" How, in other words, can we break through
our radical differences over experience?

Because this is the crucial question it admits of no facile
reply. There are those who blame philosophers for encouraging agnosticism on the score that their question-asking is
inimical to the spirit of faith and destructive of the religious
attitude of humble docility. Historically, there is some justification for this censure, since one can readily form the
impression, which only closer study can revise, that philosophers "from the first" opposed religion. Plato, for example, has always been sweet music to the ears of rationalists
because of his concentrated attacks on the "forms of theology" found in the works of the poets. He was offended, as
were several of the Greek playwrites, by the crude anthropomorphisms of the Homeric pantheon and objected to the
dissemination of these disedifying exploits. It is in this
context of a purgative atheism that we should locate his
rationalistic thrust, for he was bent on subjecting a particular form of popular religion to the mind's restraint by
"fixing the general forms in which the poets cast their tales,

and the limits which should be observed by them."[1] Even before his time, however, the tension between philosophy and religion had been mounting because of the peculiar status of the tutelary gods of the polis. The pre-Socratic philosophers of the sixth century, by their pursuit and isolation of a first principle, whether material or spiritual, had stirred the question of the relationship between this principle and the traditional civic deities. To their skeptical probings one might add the Pythagorean speculations on the nature of the soul and its destiny and the relentless interrogations of the fifth-century Sophists. The antimony of individual and city was steadily heightened—Sophocles' *Antigone* accurately reflects it—with the result that the trend away from the civic gods was alarmingly hastened. The process instigated against Anaxagoras in 432 B.C. can be viewed as a conservative effort to dam an atheistic flood. Hence it can also be classed with the charge of impiety leveled against Diagoras, against Socrates, almost certainly against Protagoras, and threatened against Aristotle in 322. All were manifestations of an outraged civic sense and the fear that unless this heresy were punished, the gods would wreak vengeance upon the city. The menace of the philosophers was simply that they shook people's confidence in the established order of things. Their questions suggested the possibility of a different experience; and whoever has the boldness to piece things together differently is guilty of unraveling the whole religious–political–social fabric.

How different experience or "the world" can be is clearly illustrated for the Christian in the narrative of Saint Paul's frustrating attempt to preach the Christian God to the Greeks gathered on the hill of the Areopagus. Paul's audience was not militantly atheist or anti-religious. But it was blind, as he later wrote to the Romans, to *the* (i.e. Pauline) world because it apparently had no background of experience for anything other than a cosmic deity. Because Paul's

1. *Republic,* II, 379a.

message was centered around a "sign to be spoken against" and the freedom that he advocated argued that his Christianity was not founded upon apodictic proofs, the acceptance of his word required a radical conversion. Greek intransigence was less a hostility to Jesus than an incapacity to entertain a personal, dying god. In this Stoic milieu "God" meant the Order, Form, or Meaning that penetrated the entire world with its influence and prevented the cosmos from reverting to chaos. Hence it was on the basis of this experience—should we say secular or religious?—that the Greek philosophers, as Saint Augustine remarked, erected a system of thought similar in aim to that of the Christians: the pursuit of a happy life.

> Listen first to the common aim of all philosophers. It is characteristic of all philosophers that, through their study, inquiry, discussion, their very life, they have sought to come to possess a happy life. This alone was the cause of philosophizing. Furthermore, I think that even this search the philosophers have in common with us.[2]

But with a heterogeneous experience to be reasoned, they evidently arrived at a divergent rational system. "The philosophers," Augustine warned, "have laid out for themselves ways of error. Some have said: this is the way. Others have said: no, not that, but this. The way was hidden from them, for God resists the proud."[3] Neither a Christian starting-point controlled their reasoning—"Unless you believe, you will not understand"—nor a Christian methodology—"Through love we ask, through love we seek, through love we knock, through love it is revealed to us, and through love we shall rest in what shall have been revealed."[4]

2. *Sermon CL*, 3, 4; in Migne's *Patrologia Latina*, XXXVIII, 309.
3. *Sermon CL*, 8, 10; *PL*, XXXVIII, 814.
4. *De Moribus Ecclesiae Catholicae*, I, 17, 31; in Migne, XXXII, 1324.

It is within this Christian, Augustinian context of thought or experience that the celebrated "ontological" argument of Saint Anselm of Canterbury belongs. Not only did the Saint commence with a prayer for light—that his striving for truth might be guided by Him Who is Truth[5]—but borrowed his antagonist, the fool, from the psalmist and then sprinkled his text with biblical citations. But more important than these merely external signs of Augustinianism is the dynamism of the argument itself. It unfolds in a perspective of unity, where the "objective" world is not an independent "out there" but a subject-related *cosmos*, an ordered and intelligible reality. Its intellectual undercurrent is the Plotinian description of the movement toward the One:

> In the advancing stages of Contemplation rising from that in Nature, to that in the Soul and thence again to that in the Intellectual Principle itself, the object contemplated becomes progressively a more and more intimate possession of the Contemplating Beings, more and more one with them; and in the advanced Soul the objects of knowledge, well on the way towards the Intellectual Principle, are close to identity with their container.

> Hence we may conclude that, in the Intellectual-Principle itself, there is complete identity of Knower and Known, and this not by way of domiciliation, as in the case of even the highest soul, but by Essence, by the fact that, there, no distinction exists between Being and Knowing; we cannot stop at a principle containing separate parts; there must always be a yet higher, a principle above all such diversity.[6]

5. Augustine's argument for the existence of God in *De Libero Arbitrio* consists in a movement from truth to Truth.
6. Plotinus, *The Enneads,* 3rd rev. ed. Eng. trans. Stephen MacKenna (London, Faber & Faber), p. 245.

In the history of proofs for God, Anselm's argument is a critical watershed. Descartes, Spinoza, Leibniz, and Hegel found it convincing, at least to the degree that they modeled arguments upon it. And in some contemporary circles, it is asserted that the "ontological argument" is the only valid proof for God. On the other hand, Thomas Aquinas rejected it on Aristotelian principles.[7] Kant, who had Descartes' version in mind rather than Anselm's, reduced all proofs for God to this argument which he declared invalid. Schopenhauer labeled it a "charming joke." Today, for sure, we are more sensitive to the fact that Anselm has been used by thinkers in accord with their personal perspectives. Yet it is surprising, given his Neoplatonic context, that a revaluation of his work has been undertaken by a group of philosophers who have rigorously analyzed his use of 'contingent,' 'necessary,' and 'existence.'[8] It behooves us, therefore, to examine closely the argument's Platonic structure in the hope of gaining some insight into the muddled question of adequate criteria of proof.

At the end of the passage from Plotinus cited above is an assertion of the isomorphism of Thought and Being, a principle that Heidegger has singled out as the hallmark of Greek thought. Undeniably the hinge of Saint Anselm's argument is the dictum of Parmenides which was a commonplace of Greek and medieval thought: Τὸ γὰρ αὐτὸ νοεῖν ἐστίν τε καὶ εἶναι: "it is the same object which is thought and which is." In a minimal sense, the principle merely reiterates the notion that thought is constituted by "like knowing like." But more comprehensively, it enunciates a theory of science or knowledge that controlled the

7. Anselm is not mentioned by name in *Summa Theologiae*, I, q.2, a.1, ad 2. For an interesting contemporary appraisal, see Gareth Matthews, "Aquinas on Saying That God Doesn't Exist," *The Monist*, 47 (1963), 472–77.
8. See the collection, Alvin Plantinga, ed., *The Ontological Argument: From St. Anselm to Contemporary Philosophers* (Garden City, N.Y., Doubleday Anchor Books, 1965).

meaning of thought and argument until the cataclysm of the Cartesian revolution. As a consequence, Anselm could reply to Gaunilo, as would Descartes at a later date, that it is a misunderstanding of the nature of thought to suppose that he is arguing from mere concepts to actual existence. Something does not exist merely because we think it. Rather, because thinking is our way of being, we shatter all the possibilities of intelligence, including fundamental concepts like "world," "man," "mind," and "reality" when we tamper with our existential relationship to things. The supposition that man stands "in the open," we would say today, underlies all human language and activity.

In Greek thought man's knowing posture was described in terms of vision.[9] In Plato's works, for instance, the sage contemplated. He grasped the existence, the being, of a present object in an immediate intuition. Basically, he understood because he "saw." Yet he obviously did not see the causes of things, those permanent, unchanging principles in the flux of experience that generate our understanding, with the eye of corporeal vision (Plato can scarcely be thought an empiricist). Nor did he infer these principles from the data of empirical experience (Aristotle's empirical starting-point necessitated his labeling the Ideas hypostatized abstractions). But he readily turned to the Ideas wherein he enjoyed a comprehensive vision of the systematic ordering of reality. Thus the Platonic doctrine of Forms was only a more sophisticated version of the traditional isomorphism, since the notion of *theoria* at the basis of the Forms was built upon the homogeneity of knowing subject and object known. Plato spoke of these Forms as present to man's soul in its pre-empirical existence so that it was by virtue of this primordial contemplation that further dialectical movement was possible. For this reason, we are entitled to look upon the Platonic knower as funda-

9. For seminal ideas of this section I am indebted to A. J. Festugière, *Contemplation et vie contemplative selon Platon* (2nd ed. Paris, Vrin, 1950).

mentally a mystic. His belief in the reality of the Ideas was contingent upon his "experience" of them. The importance of calling attention to the radical mysticism of Plato's thought is twofold. First, we must appreciate the problems resolved by the postulate of isomorphism if we are not to dismiss Anselm's argument, as did Aquinas and Kant, as an illegitimate transition from the logical or conceptual order to the real or existential order. Second, we will have to consider the issue of mysticism or "experience" in order to talk about Anselm's argument as a proof. Is Karl Barth right in the Kierkegaardian twist he has given to Saint Anselm, so that we ought not to speak about proving a fact but about explicating a belief?

Regarding the first point, we are apt to voice our appreciation of the ingenuity of Plato's theory as a solution (less dogmatically, a "theoretical answer") to the problem that Plato raised in the *Meno* and has vexed Piaget and his school of genetic psychology. Today we would phrase it: How does one learn the categories and criteria of thought? Granted that we communicate successfully, that in spite of the sophistication of Wittgenstein's hypothetical children we do learn what trees, horses, houses, and so on, are through the ambiguous process of ostensive definition, the theoretical question remains how we learn to experience or identify the world successfully within a given milieu when we have not as yet learned its accepted categories. Organization teaches us to experience, and yet experience teaches us how to organize. Having pondered the problem in his *De Magistro,* Anselm's master, Saint Augustine, replied in a typically "Platonic" way: since no one can really teach us anything, Christ must be our interior teacher. This answer has the merit of minimizing a surd. It satisfies the mind by postulating an answer whose plausibility is tested by reference to a whole context of experience. In this respect, modern scientific procedure is no different.

It would appear, then, that in the Greek world this problem of learning criteria was resolved by the declaration that the world was as the Greek saw it; those who did not, or could not, see it that way were barbarians. The possibility of Riemann's emendations to Euclid's geometry was not entertained, so that there was no reason to suppose the feasibility of another mode of "seeing." Thus the thesis of isomorphism was not an invitation to an anti-intellectual solipsism or a modern subjectivism. Because it grew out of a world of communication, it was always subject to the laws of an intersubjective world. It merely asserted that if the world is not as we apprehend it, we can never really know what "it" is. On this substantial ground Anselm built his argument.

We should note before turning to our second point that whatever the differences between Aristotelian and Platonic thought (the two viable systems open to Christian thinkers), the thesis of isomorphism was unchanged. Aristotle's forms were the forms of things, not Kantian categories. Therefore he was untroubled by the question why the mind abstracts this form rather than that.

Let us now take up the more involved question of the nature of Anselm's proof in the context of Karl Barth's reading. It is clear, I believe, that Barth's discussion is primarily a theological one. It was intended to bolster his thesis that "natural theology" was a contradiction in terms. A theology defined as God's word to man must for that very reason be revealed or supernatural. To pretend otherwise is to run the risk of Pelagianism, to reduce the God of Abraham, Isaac, and Jacob to a philosophical abstraction, and to surrender the Protestant gift principle of salvation for a Catholic position on works. Naturally, with a theological background of Luther and Schleiermacher, understood in the philosophical vocabulary of Kant and Kierkegaard, and faced with decrees of the first Vatican Council that appeared to scuttle the negative theology of the Pseudo-Denis and Hilary of Poitiers in favor of a philosophical rationalism,

Barth reacted vehemently. It has proved a stimulating reaction. For Barth was joined by many of his contemporaries,
notably by Paul Tillich and Emil Brunner, in his main
issue, which Brunner has indicated as primarily an anthropological question stemming from opposing theological
evaluations of man. Thus:

> This is the point at which the doctrine of the Reformers
> diverges from that of the Catholic Church, in accor-
> dance with their differing views of the sinful corruption
> of man. The Reformation doctrine remains strictly in
> harmony with the teaching of the Bible; it maintains
> the general revelation, but it denies that there is a
> natural "knowledge of God," which is no other than
> the dialectic of sin itself: namely, that man could not
> be a sinner if he knew nothing of God, but that on the
> other hand, precisely because he is a sinner, and in so
> far as he is a sinner he remains isolated, he cannot
> know God aright.[10]

Although of late Barth has been shown to contradict the
older Protestant theologians,[11] his influence upon Roman
Catholics has been healthy. They have been stimulated to
rethink the problems that vexed Saint Anselm in his *Epis-
tola de Incarnatione Verbi:* How is it that a rational argument can fail to convince a "fool," that is, the unbeliever?
In their deliberations many Catholics have gone back
through Blondel and Newman to Anselm and Augustine,
acknowledging that there is a point to Marcel's remark that
theodicy is an atheism, yet without committing themselves
to the theological premises of the Barthian fideism.[12] They

10. Emil Brunner, *Revelation and Reason: The Christian Doctrine of
Faith and Knowledge,* Eng. trans. Olive Wyon (Philadelphia, The Westminster Press, 1946), p. 65.
11. See Erik Schmidt, *Hegels Lehre von Gott* (Gütersloh, C. Bertelsmann
Verlag, 1952), pp. 112–13.
12. *Journal Métaphysique* (1914), 65. An English translation, *The Metaphysical Journal,* has been made by Bernard Wall (Chicago, Henry Regnery,

have been more inclined, in keeping with contemporary philosophy, to bypass cosmological arguments in favor of a theology that is deeply rooted in anthropology. "Here is the reason," Blondel wrote, "why it can be said that proofs for God are less an invention than an inventory, less a revelation than an elucidation, a purification and justification of the fundamental beliefs of humanity."[13] We can discover how this is so by focusing on two aspects of Saint Anselm's proof.

Central to the Anselmian argument is the notion of the "perfect," an idea suggestive of Plato's treatment of the Good in the *Republic*, but one that in its Greek form, τέλειος, conveys the meaning of "finished," "whole," or "complete." Thus by the choice of this term Anselm indicated that what his proof described was the dynamism of thought itself. There must be an ultimate, a whole or totality in terms of which parts are understood as finite, imperfect, and participating, because we grasp things only within contexts or structures. "A piece of wood," "an idol," "the queen in chess": each has meaning in terms of a particular structure. And so, if this is how we understand, it follows, as the Greeks maintained, that the impossibility of an infinite series is its unintelligibility. Reason, in the Kantian terminology, is guided by dialectical ideals: the world, soul, and God, the last of which is the ideal of total intelligibility that charges the mind to its unifying function. God, in other words, is implied in the everyday human presumption of truth, a contention that renders intelligible Nietzsche's vitriolic excoriation of the Platonism of Western thought.

1952). Marcel's position is clearly not Kierkegaard's. See his *Du refus à l'invocation,* esp. Chapter 9: Eng. trans. Robert Rosthal, *Creative Fidelity* (New York, Farrar, Straus, 1964), pp. 175–83.

13. Maurice Blondel, *La Pensée* (Paris, Presses Universitaires de France, 1934), *1,* 396.

In choosing a proof that moved within the dialectic of knowledge, Anselm by that very fact placed himself within the context of Greek philosophical religion. It was a commonplace of Greek thought that the divinity of the gods consisted in their contemplation of, and nourishment by, the Ideas. As Plato noted of his predecessors, Anaximenes described his air, Heraclitus his fire, Anaximander the *apeiron,* Xenophanes his One-Whole, and Empedocles his sphere as *theos* or *theion.* God, unlike the representations of the popular mythology, was a name for the supreme intelligible, the ultimate law of reality, the Whole or One in terms of which parts were seen as significantly related. Philosophy, accordingly, even for Plato, was a religious way of life, a path, as Augustine warned, to divinization. It entailed catharsis and conversion since one must undergo an ascesis or discipline in order to "see" into things more deeply. Thus the pursuit of truth was a moral act because science was a *mystique.* Knowledge shone with the aureole of virtue.

For Karl Barth, the idea of using the dialectic of knowledge in this way—as Henri Duméry and others have done in our times—was anathema because it reduced the God of the Judaeo-Christian revelation to an ultimate Greek principle. Consequently, his sympathy for Kant inclined him to pinpoint Anselm's peculiar notion of existence: one that Kant lampooned in his example of a hundred real as opposed to a hundred imaginary dollars and that is discussed today in terms of existence as a predicate. It is important in the light of our previous remarks about isomorphism that we recognize that to discuss Saint Anselm exclusively in these terms is simply to miss the point, even though we might grant that his Neoplatonic *Weltanschauung* led him to talk about existence as another tag, another perfection, that the Most Perfect must have as the summation of all perfections. Indeed, the anomalies of this type of thought were still around to plague Saint Thomas, whose works portray the various stages of his wrestling with the consequent difficulty of reconciling divine omniperfection with absolute simplicity.

Rather than be paralyzed by Barth's horror of reductionism, an emotion that is understandable in view of the history of the Enlightenment, can we not look for benefits from the Greek philosophical technique of proving God by an explication of the presuppositions of thought? Are we not far enough away from the Enlightenment to risk the accusation of reductionism, especially since the Barthian alternative is an anti-intellectual fideism? Barthians must be negative toward the Greeks and hostile to philosophy, whereas bona fide followers of Saint Anselm, if I interpret him correctly, would share Aquinas' enthusiasm for the achievement of the Greek argumentation to "what we call God" and his conviction that a faith uprooted from its rational groundings must inevitably wither. The point, however, that any believer must concede to Barth is clear: that the Greek philosophical God was only an intimation, not a revelation, of the God of Judaism and Christianity. It was essentially a cosmic principle that needed an irruption of the normal course of events, a revelation, to be seen as a person. Greek intellectualism was incapable of reaching this point of cosmic personalism.

Moreover, it must be confessed that Barth, following Kierkegaard, has raised a significant issue by probing Saint Anselm's starting-point. Ostensibly, he has argued that the believer needs no proof for God (the requirement of a theodicy betrays at least an incipient atheism) and that the unbeliever lacks the proper structure for appreciating such an argument. Consequently, Anselm's argument is a tour de force. Since the Saint began within the confines of faith, the argument can hardly be dignified as a proof; its persuasiveness extends only to those who accept its premises.

Contemporary philosophers might supply additional information that would enhance the formidableness of this objection. Still they would not on that account declare that we can no longer talk about proof. Without shared premises, no one can prove anything to anybody since the logic of argument is nothing but consistency within an adopted system. The real problem of proof, then, is to engender the experience requisite for making a proof meaningful.[14] Thus, like anyone else who constructs an argument, Saint Anselm believed that he had fashioned a proof that was universal in scope; anyone who thinks—barring, therefore, the fool—should be compelled by its force. All of us are guilty of projecting our norms and talking as it were for all times and places. Certainly the Greeks did, and so did the *Aufklärer*. But this does not mean, surely, that we have forgotten the paradox of our universality, our essential temporal and spatial relatedness. Nor does our acceptance of this fact commit us to a devastating philosophical relativism, the view, namely, that nothing human can be "true." On this score, philosophers who are sensitive to the historicity of man that results from his incarnation never fail to en-

---

14. This point has been recognized by Henri de Lubac, *Sur les chemins de Dieu* (Paris, Aubier, 1956), p. 105. Karl Rahner in "Wissenschaft als Konfession?" *Wort und Wahrheit, 11* (1954), 812, has expressed it vividly:

The terror in the face of the absence of God from the world, the feeling of no longer being able to realize the divine, the consternation before the silence of God, before a God who seems to shut himself up in his inaccessibility, before a world becoming profane and empty of meaning, before the mute and impersonal objectivity of cosmic laws, even when it is no longer a question of "nature" but of man—this experience, which often thinks itself obliged to interpret itself theoretically as atheism, is an authentic experience of the depths of existence . . . with which the thought and current manner of speaking in Christianty will for a long time yet have to explain itself. But this is only, at bottom, the experience that God is not a part of the picture of the world . . . It is, then, only the evolution of the idea of God in the spirit of humanity. Today we are experiencing anew, and in a more radical way than ever before, something which we have already known in the abstract, thanks to the Vatican Council, but which we have not taken with sufficient seriousness: God is inexpressibly beyond all creation and can be thought apart from it.

counter the objections of theologians. Perhaps the real difficulty lies with the theologians who have been mesmerized by their talk about eternal truths.

Personally, I feel that Barth was less concerned about the logic of Saint Anselm's starting-point than he was troubled by the commitments the Saint made when he bound himself to the patterns of Greek thought. If, for example, Bishop Robinson accepts the premises of empiricism or Harvey Cox the outlook of Comte, are they not logically committed to certain conclusions that might prove inimical to their theology? If nothing else, philosophical systems are rigorously logical; one "buys" the whole Hume or Kant or Hegel when he accepts without reservation the first lines of their works. In like manner, the difficulty of systematic theology since the time of Augustine has been this web-like feature of one's adopted philosophy. Could it be that Barth sensed a compromise in Anselm's reliance on Greek reflective and probative techniques?

Greek thought was, as we have seen, holistic in scope. In Plotinus, whom Augustine and Anselm refashioned for their purposes, thought was described as a double dialectical movement: an ascent to the One, the Absolute that terminates our unifying activity but cannot itself be thought since thinking involves otherness or duality, and a descent from the One as the principle in which all things are seen as intelligible. This thrust toward totality became a feature of the philosophy of religion—here I will assert only that it was due to the holistic nature of the religious experience itself—one that contributed to making it both a satisfying and a disturbing experience. It was satisfying because everything was set in its proper place and duly accounted for, disturbing because it introduced a pantheism or panentheism into Christian thought that has never been completely exorcized. We need only think of the philosophers Spinoza and Hegel or of Père de Lubac's spirited defense of Teilhard de Chardin (in which texts of the Fathers are resorted to as elaborations of Saint Paul's expressions: God is "all in all," the one "in whom we live, move, and have our being") in order to appreciate Santayana's observation: the choice lies between the philosophies of Spinoza and Thomas Aquinas. Undoubtedly it is hazardous to present a dialectic of transcendence and immanence, of finite and infinite, of limited and pure act, without one of the correlatives disappearing. The danger to Christianity in this heady intellectualism is that a thrust toward complete unification is readily transformed into a movement of absolute unicity. Plotinus, in other words, remains unchanged despite his Christian apparel.

Saint Augustine was aware that Greek philosophy required revamping if it was to serve his Christian purposes. The most evident change that had to be made was in the theory of emanation, for if the ascents and descents of the One were necessary movements, it would follow for the Christian that God had to create. But the entire Christian dispensation was built on a gift of love and its implied idea of freedom. The question, then, was how one is to reconcile the necessary connection of causality with the freedom of divine liberality. Surely, if by explanation we uncover only necessary connections, are we not given over to a world of determinism? We might note in passing how, in the wake of the rejection of the medieval Christian synthesis, this question returned to agitate Hume and Kant. The snare of an intellectualist philosophy has always been to minimize or suppress talk about will by referring to it as irrational passion or emotion.

Our interest is not to detail all of the distinctions utilized by Christian thinkers to circumvent this difficulty. Rather, it is to indicate clearly that what these Christians did, Anselm among them, was to loosen the rigor of the process of inference. In Wittgenstein's language, they softened the "hardness of the logical 'must' " by showing that the model of a neat hypothetico-deductive system could not be the paradigm for inferences in religious thought. Logic, they implicitly argued, had to be more than what Aristotle described, and for that they continue to be impugned by critics of a scientific cast of mind. This point is sufficiently important to warrant elucidation.

It is the current fashion to attribute Aristotle's objections against Platonism to a difference in temperament. His biological preference led him to depict knowledge as taking wing upon abstraction from empirical data. If science was contemplative at all, it appeared so only consequently, not antecedently. Hence abstraction superceded confrontation as the initial act of the mind, so that thinking became the activity of subsuming "matter" under "forms," truth was an affair of valid inference (when consistency becomes the matrix of truth, one naturally becomes preoccupied with the laws of the syllogism), and science comprised the system of forms, that is, the complete or total view of the interrelations of things. In this way the theory of abstraction led inexorably to the notion of science as a classificatory system—to the student of modern philosophy these notions will be familiar because of Kant—so that it was natural for Aristotle to make significant use of the biological category of genus in his philosophical writings.

If I may borrow terms pertinent to the philosophy of science, we might suggest that the Aristotelian temperament favors the logic of discovery. One notes connections in his empirical observation, develops a theory of causality, and, as in the case of Saint Thomas, extrapolates from the immediate data to discuss the cause of "the world." It is a method that postpones the critical question until the end, for the "surd" of what constitutes or regulates data is not faced until the end of the process. Its strong point is its deductive rigor; its weakness—evidenced, to a degree, by the charge of heresy leveled against Aquinas and the fruits produced by Descartes—a mode of thinking that appears antithetical to religion. Perhaps we have here an answer to the question why we do not have a scientific philosophy of religion.

By contrast, the Platonic mentality of Augustine and Anselm may be thought to favor a logic of explication. One begins his reflection *en situation,* with a recognition of his existential location in a world of belief. His logic starts from the "surd" of a whole milieu, the fact that one finds himself in a world with these particular categories and commitments at hand. His inferences frankly consist in explicating his initial stance, as opposed to an inductive procedure that accosts "parts" without knowing them as such. The method's strong point lies precisely in its acceptance of this "surd" of one's initial position; its weak point is that "giving reasons" ("rational explanations" William Dray has called them in his elaboration of the logic of history)[15] lacks the logical tautness of strict deduction. One's exploration has the guise of promoting, not challenging, the *status quo.*

The logic of explication can be defended as a tool for the philosophy of religion not merely because it has been used successfully in the past (insofar as it offers a type of thought congenial to the religious experience) but also because it takes into account the world as religiously committed people affirm it to be. Christians asseverate that man's existential situation is one of grace, so that concepts like "natural order" or "natural reason" are acknowledged to be merely conceptual devices that allow them to talk about the actual order of things. Consequently, Barth was right in asserting that Anselm had to begin in belief. But he was wrong in supposing that an argument beginning from that starting-point might not qualify as a proof. It does not, of course, if one insists that a proof must be constructed according to a logic of discovery. We can be forthright about a difference of rigor in these two modes of argumentation: the one has

15. See especially his *Laws and Explanations in History* (Oxford, at the University Press, 1957).

the absoluteness of intellectualism, the other permits the openness of freedom. This latter employs the criterion: Does this way of explaining make things more intelligible? It is a norm, I would suggest, that befits our ecumenical age; for without it, must we not brand dissenters to our logic as either stupid or malicious?

At this point it is my hope that the reader has not been discouraged by the somewhat eccentric turn that our discussion of Saint Anselm has taken. For it was my purpose to touch upon several points that might help us to understand his argument, specifically, the Platonic movement of his thought, the idea of knowledge as *theoria* (a looking that is a total or comprehensive view), and the peculiar logic of his proof. I have brought these notions into a context of Karl Barth's treatment of the Saint both because his position has been the focal point of considerable contemporary debate, and because its arguments betray his personal theological and denominational commitments as well as the peculiar view of man that underlies them. He shows us unmistakably that we argue from a total point of view.

The thrust of this chapter, therefore, has been toward suggesting that questions of any kind are in reality questionings. Our diverse forms of interrogation, religious included, relate directly to the canons of satisfying modes of proof. Thus man's experience of the world as a whole—in the context, that is, of a given society—forms the matrix of his reasoning. In this way, all genuine thought is actually self-appropriation. Wherefore, Marcel's objections to theodicy do not constitute a Barthian fideism. Rather, they are calls for explication: the outcome of a vivid realization that most arguments and formulae are like icebergs seen from the surface. Why? Because they are elucidations, purifications, and justifications of the fundamental beliefs of humanity. Theology, too, as a questioning enterprise, must find its deepest roots in anthropology.

The following two chapters on Descartes and Hume are

markedly anthropological in orientation and dictated by hermeneutical interests. Since in this chapter we have raised the question of the starting-point of one's investigations, in the next chapter we shall focus upon the human Ego. The intention is to explore the kind of thought that has located man's principles of interpretation in subjective consciousness.

THREE. CONSTITUTION OF AND
BY THE EGO

In us, as in a flint, are the seeds of knowledge,
which the philosophers educe by reasoning
but which the poets shake out and make scin-
tillate by the power of imagination.

DESCARTES, *Cogitationes Privatae*

It is regrettable that for popular consumption contemporary
philosophers have found it convenient to label the Cartesian
position with the catchy but disparaging tag, the myth of
the ghost in the machine. We are easily captivated by the
glitter of the phrasemaker's truth and perhaps never notice
the tarnish that inevitably accumulates through prolonged
exposure. Once familiarity has been substituted for insight,
we are in danger of seizing upon this catch phrase to serve
a polemical intent. As a consequence, the true significance,
the abiding reality, of Descartes is obscured. The safeguard
is to remind ourselves at intervals that the new mentality
of the seventeenth century exceeded in importance the new
science, if only because we have still to come to terms with
the problem of the Cartesian method: whether truth is
disclosed in the form of a systematic and total vision of the
universe or, so to speak, distributed in a multitude of
propositions.

If the claim is true that since Descartes humanity has
thought with a view to truth rather than from a starting-
point in truth, we cannot attribute this fact uniquely to his
peculiar genius. Notwithstanding his pretense of having
swept away the past and started afresh, Descartes, as we
know, stood solidly upon the shoulders of ancestral giants.
Scholars have compiled an index that testifies his indebted-

ness to the Scholastics; the influence of the Oratory, notably
Cardinal de Bérulle himself, has been suggested as the
source of his Augustinianism; his texts are sprinkled with
"wind," "light," and other commonplace Renaissance philosophical terms; a similar interest in method can be found
in personalities as diverse as Bacon, Hobbes, Grotius, and
some representative Spanish scholastics. When we place
Descartes' methodology of the mind in its historical setting,
we can better understand his spirit: it is insufficient to have
a good mind; the principal thing is that one apply it well.
People had not yet gotten over the cataclysm of the previous
century that had shaken all the old securities: the Church,
the State, the Bible; and in the intellectual world, the humanism that had been intended to supplant a sterile scholasticism failed to offer a viable philosophy for men groping
through the problems of the new science. Indeed, if there
had been no Descartes, his world would have invented one.
Montaigne's skepticism was symptomatic of these ills. To
remedy them, Pierre Charron suggested a fideism, Francis
Bacon proposed experience (a suggestion that we will consider in the next chapter), whereas Descartes' panacea was
to analyze the mind, since this was tantamount to defining
the exact nature and scope of human knowledge or truth.

For our interest, Descartes' overt religious declarations
and the scholarly controversy these have occasioned need
not detain us.[1] Of primary import, however, is the gener-

1. Jacques Maritain *(The Dream of Descartes,* Eng. trans. M. L. Andison [New York, Philosophical Library, 1944]) has called attention to the
embarrassment of philosophers because of the cerebral episode and vow to
visit the shrine of Our Lady at Loretto at the origin of "modern philosophy."
But the major dispute has been over reconciling the obvious rationalistic
spirit of Descartes' writings with his protestations of loyalty to the Church.
There is, certainly, no lack of verbal religious testimony. Descartes was
always careful to cultivate his former Jesuit instructors; he dedicated the
Meditations, in which he "demonstrated" the existence of God, to the dean
and professors of the faculty of theology at Paris; and he assured his faithful
correspondent, Père Mersenne: "Je ne voudrais pour rien au monde qu'il
sortit de moi un discours où il se trouvât le moindre mot qu'il fût désap-

ating idea of his reflection: that the human mind, like a piece of flint, was a "something" governed by definite laws. The fruit of meditating upon it would not be an insight into its inherent structure in the sense that one would grasp its "components," but that he would have the "feel" that he was following its laws, as it were striking the flint with the requisite "know-how," because of the brilliance—the clarity and distinctness—of his sparks or ideas. In Descartes' theory, the important element was not *what* one thinks but *how,* that is, whether one experienced that force or subjective impact which carried with it the guarantee that he was thinking in conformity with the mind's laws and therefore truly.

Admittedly, it is not germane to our purpose to follow the movement of Descartes' thought from beginning to end; from his starting-point in the universal experience of human error, through his discrimination of various kinds of ideas, to his eventual subsumption of the body and the world under the Cogito. These notions have been amply explicated and criticized by philosophers from Descartes' day to our own. But it is pertinent for us to take note of the lure of his common-sense appeal and the momentous supposition accompanying it. "I then proceeded to consider in a general manner," he tells us in the *Discours,*

what is requisite to the truth and certainty of a proposition. Having found one—"I think therefore I am"—

prouvé de l'Eglise." Consequently, Laberthonnière, Gilson, Gouhier, and other commentators have regarded Descartes as sincerely religious, although they have recognized that his "love of tranquility" might have accounted for his protestations of loyalty. M. Leroy, on the other hand, has borrowed an expression from the juvenile *Praeambula,* "larvatus prodeo," in order to show in two volumes (*M. Descartes, le philosophe au masque,* [Paris, Riedler, 1929]) that Descartes' mask was a religious front. In view of the "novelty" of Descartes' ideas, it seems better to interpret his maneuverings as signs of caution, as did Bossuet, whom Maritain has cited (p. 42): "M. Descartes has always been afraid of being reprimanded by the Church, and to avoid that, he is known to take excessive precautions."

that I knew to be true and certain, I thought that I
ought also to know in what this certainty consists; and
having noted that in this proposition nothing assures
me of its truth save only that *I see very clearly* that *in
order to think* it is necessary to be, I judged that I could
take as being a general rule that the things we apprehend very clearly and distinctly are true.[2]

It was the commonplace assurance that "even if I am not
sure about anything else, at least I can be sure of myself,
that is, of my existence," which launched Descartes' search
for the ingredients of certitude. His intuition—for he never
asserted his "therefore" as a formal illation—was simply a
synthesis of the prerequisites of thought that he had detected. In order to think one must not only be but also, and
more importantly, be convinced that he can be sure. Rationality demands certainty, for we think in order to grasp,
to comprehend, to make something our own. It is this process of comprehension, in popular speech "knowledge" or
"science," that affords man (qua rational animal) his basic
security in the world. Without security—in Descartes'
terms, if the mind errs about everything, even about its most
clear and distinct ideas—there is no truth, no science, no
point of insertion into, or relation to, a world.

In keeping with the Augustinian–Anselmian philosophical tradition, Descartes presented his arguments for God
within this dialectic of knowledge. But a different spirit
moved him. God was a presumption of truth in a way that
was alien to Saint Anselm's initial philosophical postulate.
Since this difference marks the change in mind and attitude
of the new age of science, an age that saw a complete reshap-
ing of the philosophy of religion, it is imperative that we
take notice of its characteristics and savor its novelties.

Significantly, most discussions of Descartes on God drift

2. *René Descartes: Discours de la Méthode, texte et commentaire,* Étienne
Gilson, ed. (2nd ed. Paris, Vrin, 1939), p. 31. Italics added.

away from the actual arguments as they are found in the Third and Fifth Meditations in order to concentrate on God's function as a guarantor of human certitude. If Rationality requires certainty, as Descartes maintained, then evidently the Greek thesis of isomorphism remains intact. In Spinoza's language, the order and connection of ideas is the order and connection of things. Yet for Descartes this fact was secondary. Certainly he never denied that the real world was a world of logical implication—"Nature acts in everything mathematically"—but the actual focal point of his interest was the psychological impact of ideas, not their content. Consequently, primordial in his thinking was the fact that God guaranteed minds by permitting men to have clear and distinct ideas, although contained within this guarantee was ideational truth, that is, a correspondence to reality. The thrust of Descartes' thought was that God has failed if there is something wrong with our thinking apparatus, if *He,* we should note, deceives us by allowing us to assume the truth of our clear and distinct ideas when in fact they are false.

Two points emerge from this description of Descartes' procedure. First, the basis of Nietzsche's condemnation of Western philosophy is apparent. The Cartesian presumption of truth does depend ultimately upon the existence of God. Second, even though Descartes offered an ontological argument suggestive of Anselm (one that paved the way for Kant's refutation because of its setting in a radical mind–world dichotomy), the sense of the argument—that God alone could have given man his idea of the perfect—was that were it not for divine goodness, the operations of the human mind would be fallible. This, I would suggest, is the real paradox of the Cartesian religious position. The medievals, who stood in the Greek tradition, could argue that God is implied in the activity of thought on the grounds that He is the Whole or Totality, in virtue of which parts of the world are seen as intelligible parts. God was implied in the truth of the world simply because the world was "seen" as a unified whole: an ordered, that is to say, intelligible (not necessarily totally rational or rationalized) system. Descartes, on the contrary, divorced his proof of God from this holistic vision. Because he assumed the order of the world in order to emphasize that God is implied in the proper performance of the mind in its quest for certitude, how could he argue to God either by a logic of explication or by a logic of discovery? Evidently, the refusal of the holistic vision, a starting-point in truth, excluded a logic of explication. On the other hand, how was the piecemeal approach of a logic of discovery, which Descartes' methodology canonized, to lead to God? If thinking "with a view to truth" is by definition a search for norms, it is questionable that its results, which can never be definitive, have a right to be called truths. Consequently, the presumption of truth in the Cartesian scheme was radically different from that in the Greek and medieval tradition. By comparison, Descartes' appears to be a "pure presumption," since the vision of the Greeks, as Hegel pointed out, had the merit of guaranteeing itself. Its supposition of truth is justified in the gradual unfolding of the system. For when we see how everything in our experience fits together, we can adjudge whether a scheme of cohesiveness accounts for all the data in a satisfactory way.

The enigma, then, of Descartes' stance is that he stood with one foot in the Greek world. By clinging to its tradition of rationality, he was necessarily committed to a mind–world isomorphism and its implicit epistemology. But in reaction to that tradition as it was expressed in the late Renaissance, Descartes emphasized mind or subjective factors in a way that loosened the ground beneath his feet. Justly, to be sure, he combatted the fossilized notion of tradition that idolizes authorities as if they were the court of last appeal in settling disputes. Yet his campaign for personal conviction was too narrowly conceived and as a consequence vitiated by misplaced emphases. Ironically, it contributed to the overturn of the religious viewpoint that according to the dedicatory epistle of the *Meditations* he wished to defend. Let us try to see this important point more clearly through a sharper delineation of some of the consequences of Descartes' attitude toward tradition.

It is revealing to the reader of the *Regulae,* where the deductive procedure of a *mathesis universalis* is so striking, and of the *Discours* and *Meditations,* where the project of uncovering the structures of the mind is so apparent, to reflect that Descartes' "lighthouse" theory of the mind is peculiarly anti-historical. The mind presumably casts its penetrating light upon the field of knowledge, illuminating things once and for all as they really are. We can excuse this way of talking, perhaps, on the grounds that it was a blind spot inherited from the Greeks. But its oddity is conspicuous even in the *Regulae,* where the mathematical bent of Descartes tended to make him prolix on the subject of deduction (he insisted that these inferences should as far as possible approximate the clarity of intuitions) but annoyingly reserved on the topic of intuition. Yet the entire weight of his theory rests upon the singular clarity and universality of these primary intuitions, for supposedly in them we apprehend "simple natures," the building-blocks of truth. If conclusions are the test of reasoning, Descartes obviously had to guarantee shared premises. In other words, he did not postulate an axiomatic system. His theory required something in the objective order akin to Greek eternal forms that would ensure that the mind's infallible operations terminated in unanimity. He presumed, therefore, common initial intuitions, even though this presumption eliminated a philosophical, as opposed to a voluntarist, account of a change of mind or a difference of viewpoint. We can sympathize with his concern for individual certitude, for the overpowering clarity and distinctness of one's personal ideas, but not to the degree that we condone a disregard for, or elimination of, all diversity in truth. Unfortunately, this pursuit of clarity prompted him to sweep the slate of his mind clean and start literally from scratch. As a consequence, he could accept nothing from tradition, especially any evidence that our criteria or proof and truth might be inherited from the past, having reached their present refined state through a process of evolution.

This objection has usually been voiced: Descartes' theory of the mind fosters the bogus absolutism of a subjectivism and a relativism, notions that are essentially solipsistic because of their stress on individual impression and evalution. Conversely, an historical point of view, one that catches us in the web of mankind, is of necessity one that fosters subjectivity and relativity, terms that highlight the interpersonal, societal nature of knowledge. Thus Descartes' very pattern of thought put him at loggerheads with the Christianity that he professed. Christianity has inherited from Judaism a communal life, a spirituality that of its nature was derived from, and is therefore lived in and for, "the people of God." Its adherents are nourished by its tradition, by the living Word of God as it expresses itself in the collective consciousness of the group. Its traditional theology of original sin and of redemption in Christ are dependent upon the solidarity of mankind. How, then, does one establish a common link between these themes and Descartes' rugged individualism?

More radically anti-Christian, undoubtedly, was Descartes' contention that he was a mind, not a man. Such a patently anti-incarnational opinion was voiced in direct opposition to the basic tenet of Christianity; it was, besides, the root of Descartes' anti- or transhistorical attitude. By our bodies we are situated in space and time, inserted into a determinate cultural milieu, and rendered present to others. Consequently, the disincarnate mind suffers no limitations upon its thought. Literally it is in-finite: oblivious rather than present to all times and places, an absolute norm of thought, a "pure reason." Thus in one incredible anthropological stroke Descartes undid the work of his Christian predecessors back to the times of Augustine. By making man a mind and not a human being, he extirpated that element of love they had inserted into the deleterious Greek dialectic of thought. The rationalism of the Enlightenment, with its corrections of human understanding and critiques of pure reason, was set on its course. The medieval argument for God as the terminus of the dialectic of knowledge was replaced by a Greek intellectual abstraction: God as a mere requirement of thought.

For all of his modernity, therefore, Descartes was the herald of a new breed of ancients. Paradoxically, he argued for God as a necessity of thinking without the Hellenic encumbrances of holism or isomorphism. The result was predictable. His geometrical constructionism merely emphasized that ideas or concepts like God, nature, reality, and so on, are human. We suppose that our way is the only way of ordering things because the world has been made for us by God, who would not—indeed could not—deceive us. Kant's shattering contribution, grounded on the Cartesian stance and fortified by a strong dose of Humean empiricism, was that even though we may need God to think, and must have Him to live morally, still we cannot know for sure that He is there to order our world. True, the mind relies upon an all-encompassing regulative concept, but the Cartesian method encourages us to forget this foggy transcendental ideal for clear-cut, immediate data. Hence we would do better to forget these vain epistemological, metaphysical, and theological questions and settle down to the real business of making this a better world in which to live.

It is almost a truism in philosophy that movements of thought are more important than their arguments, if only because any argument is the articulate reflection of a particularly inspired way of life. As a consequence, up to this point I have been eager to indicate how radically different

Descartes' argument for God "from the idea that we have of Him," as he informed Père Mersenne, was from Saint Anselm's similarly worded proof. That an alien spirit breathed through his thought can be witnessed from its repercussions. His idea of God, the traditional Supreme Being of Western scholasticism, became the pivotal concept of an immanentist theology which in the course of time presented itself as unadulterated anthropology. At the risk of losing our focus, let us trace the history of this Cartesian movement of interiorization primarily because it offers us the *mise-en-scène* for a host of contemporary theological problems. If present-day theologians continue to flirt with the Cartesian–Humean–Kantian pattern of thought, they cannot protest that they do not know what they are doing.

The philosophical assault on Christianty is usually dated from Gotthold Lessing, who died in 1781, the year that Kant published his first *Critique*. Lessing devoted his considerable talent and energy to a criticism of historical Christianity in order to purge it. Bizarre myths and unseemly exploits had to be purified and "spiritualized" in the same way that Plato had decreed the purgation of the Homeric poems. An historically incarnate "God with us" was incorrigibly primitive and external; to be meaningful it had to be interiorized (or de-transcendentalized) into a satisfying "God within us." It is noteworthy that not a significant writer of this period— Schiller, Goethe, Herder, Hölderlin, or Richter—however externally conformist he might have been, seems to have held on to an objectively imposing doctrine. Rational Christianity was a religion in which dogmas were forced to deliver their "true meanings," in which supernatural accounts were systematically demythologized, and in which social conformity supplanted ecclesiastical commitment. Fichte's influential *Essay Toward a Critique of All Revelation* (1792) touched a responsive chord in these Cartesian-infected intellectuals.

Within the Church itself theologians were of different minds regarding the beneficence or maleficence of the *Zeitgeist*. Many of the "old guard" were suspicious of a philosophy of practical reason, since the anthropocentric thrust of a moral philosophy seemed clearly at odds with an emphasis upon the gift-character of salvation. Yet they found some assurance in the piety of the "early" Kant and Fichte, whose works strengthened their stand on religion's role as the educator of human liberty. Inversely, many of the younger theologians, the so-called Neologens, became extreme rationalists. To them we owe the ruthless attack on the supernatural known historically as the criticism of dogma. Christ, as they spoke of him, was an uninspiring Jewish Socrates: an exponent of the dry, sermonizing moralism they found in the Sermon on the Mount. Hegel's youthful *Life of Jesus*, the reflection of his Kant-inspired seminary days, crystallized this concept.

It is a moot subject among Hegelian scholars whether this interiorizing movement of rationalism was staunched or accelerated by the mature Hegel. Proponents of his rationalism have an impressive weight of evidence in their favor. External factors, for instance the influence of Storr, his rationalistic professor of theology at Tübingen, can be brought to bear on the interpretation of his words so that contradictory statements are taken ironically or good-humoredly. Thus one of Hegel's most recent expositors has affirmed: "When he treated Christianity sympathetically, it was only to commend it as an important, if somewhat benighted, anticipation of modern philosophy."[3] Internally, the Hegelian attacks on the Kantian philosophy, specifically on the problems centered in the noumenon, are regarded as motivated by rationalistic reductionism, although some-one less committed to atheism might regard Hegel's efforts as a direct attack on a perennial romanticism or mysticism

3. Walter Kaufmann, *Hegel: Reinterpretation, Texts, and Commentary* (Garden City, N.Y., Doubleday, 1965), pp. 66, 62.

to which the Kantian philosophy had lent an air of respectability. Is there, in fact, a religion that lacks a coterie of enthusiastic believers ever ready and willing to magnify the divine transcendence and so put a premium on inconceivability and ineffability? Hegel was aware of the dangers inherent in this kind of talk. From being intellectually unapproachable, God swiftly degenerates into something "emotional," pseudo-scientific, incommunicable. Consequently, he planned a two-pronged attack on the Kantian "bad infinite." First, he would free human reason from empiricist bonds and insist that in all knowledge man finds himself, that is, discloses the rational or humanly significant in things. Thus an infinite that is not in some way assimilated to the finite is a contradiction in terms. Second, he would undercut the Kantian-oriented theologians by pointing to the example of the Incarnation. For if the finite has no openness to the infinite, revelation and incarnation, the key concepts of Christianity, are worthless. This was the sense of a remark he once made about Kant's friend, Hamann: that all of the characteristics of Christianity—dogmatics, doctrine, belief, and so on—were for him merely human. In that position, one cannot talk about a divine self-revelation.

It is not to our purpose to weigh the pros and cons for the Hegelians of the Right or Left, namely for those who esteemed Hegel as the great reconciler who restored all things in Christ or those who celebrated him as the consummate rationalist who exposed religion as a projection of the partially reflected consciousness. In a later chapter we shall return to this aspect of his thought. But it is important for the contemporary theologian to see clearly the outcome of this rationalist trend, one to which he inevitably pledges himself when he opts for a Kantian-type theology. By 1845 it looked as if the whole Christian–bourgeois world were tottering. Feuerbach had discerned the inner workings of theological minds and announced that theology is anthropology. Strauss claimed that the Gospels had their origins in the myth-making consciousness of the primitive Christian community. Bruno Bauer denied the historicity and divinity of Christ. Marx credited the success of Christianity to its promise of "pie in the sky" in compensation for the miseries of this life. Kierkegaard surrendered the incarnational, historical reality of the Church, of theology, and of the Christian State for a despairing, decisive leap of faith. The Kantian alienation of faith from knowledge had run its course. But unlike Hegel, these followers of the Left significantly chose estrangement instead of reconciliation. They preferred negation (the part) to the dialectical self-appropriation (the whole) that Hegel had fancied as the freedom or totality of the children of God.

For some distance we have followed this Cartesian-instigated movement "within" because it so clearly illustrates how a break-up of the whole man, as in Kant's knowledge–faith dichotomy, is destined to be irreligious. Moreover, it brings us naturally to our present-day concern: one that actually had its prophet in Feuerbach but is now more frequently connected with the names of Nietzsche, Freud, and Sartre.

> Religion, at least the Christian, is the relation of man to himself, or more correctly, to his own nature (i.e. his subjective nature): but a relation to it, viewed as a nature apart from his own. The divine being is nothing else than the human being, or, rather, the human nature purified, freed from the limits of the individual man, made objective, i.e. contemplated and revered as another, a distinct being. All the attributes of the divine nature, are, therefore, attributes of the human nature.[4]

Here, indeed, is a new kind of totality, a holistic thought that, unlike Descartes', does not presuppose God for its

4. Ludwig Feuerbach, *The Essence of Christianity*, Eng. trans. George Eliot (New York, Harper & Brothers, 1957), p. 14.

complete view of truth. In fact, it is a total or unified view of things only in an analogous sense, since its parts are not related to one another in the same kind of dependence–independence dialectic. It is, therefore, a unity or identity, not an actual unification. Historically, of course, it is the culmination of the Cartesian subjective thrust that had halted, momentarily at least, in Kant's rationalistic synthesis. The Kantian empiricism, to the extent that it featured scientific objectivity, de-anthropomorphized thought; and to the extent that it was mixed with pietism, exaggerated transcendence. In other words, by pausing at otherness, it braked the movement into absolute immanence. Feuerbach, however, exemplified the theological tragedy of the inward plunge. "Whoever," Barth has warned, and Buber has seconded him, "is concerned with the spirit, the heart, and conscience, and the inwardness of man must be confronted with the question of whether he is really concerned with God and not with the apotheosis of man."[5] It is a warning that must be kept in mind whenever one is inclined to take the easy step from asserting that Reason translates the theologian's God into a First Cause, Ultimate Truth, Unmoved Mover, Ground of Being, Ultimate Concern, and the like, to saying that Reason unequivocally enunciates what the theologian's God really means.

Perhaps it is not premature, notwithstanding the Kantian and other Cartesian-originated commitments of many contemporary theologians, to suppose that the era of reductionism has passed. Actually, the inward thrust of Descartes' thought has brought us to a more critical point: to a humanistic experience that consigns theology and all God-talk to irrelevance. And so, even though it is commonly said that a humanistic atheism, like that of Marx or Sartre, has been effective in uniting Christians among themselves and with other religious people, the problem remains of finding some common ground for a theistic–atheistic dialogue.

5. Barth's Introductory Essay to *The Essence of Christianity*, p. xxv.

The efforts of the Marxist, Roger Garaudy, and of the death-of-God theologians have assured us of the difficulty of this undertaking. For who of us does not lapse into silence when asked how one goes about engendering another mentality? Yet may we not suggest that theologians might find some help were they to explore those primitive beliefs of humanity mentioned in the last chapter? Surely there is more to be said about the Supreme Io of the Maori, for example, or about Ngai, the high god of the Kikuyu, than that they are "interesting fictions of primitives." For us the following description of Nzambi Mpungu, the high god of the Bakongo, may be strange; but because it articulates a human experience and synthesizes an entire outlook on life, we ought to sift it carefully for an insight into man that might correct a myopic Western viewpoint.

Nzambi Mpungu is a being, invisible, but very powerful, who has made all, men and things, even fetishes which he has given to men for their good. "If he had not given us our fetishes, we should all be dead long ago." He intervenes in the creation of every child, he punishes those who violate his prohibitions. They render him no worship, for he has need of none and is inaccessible. On earth man lives with his incessant needs to satisfy; the aged have there a privileged position. Above all is Nzambi, the sovereign Master, unapproachable, who has placed man here below to take him away some day, at the hour of death. He watches man, searches him out everywhere and takes him away, inexorably, young or old. . . . Among the laws there are *nkondo mi Nzambi,* "God's prohibitions," the violation of which constitutes a *sumu ku Nzambi* [a sin against Nzambi], and an ordinary sanction of this is *lufwa lumbi* "a bad death."[6]

6. Mircea Eliade, *From Primitives to Zen: A Thematic Sourcebook of the History of Religions* (New York & Evanston, Harper & Row, 1967), p. 6;

The striking feature of this account is its unabashed personalism: a heritage of experience that Descartes' antihistorical, anti-traditional attitude would completely suppress in us. Descartes' cast of mind has been abetted by the rationalizations of Comte and Freud, with the result that our technological advances seem to have been made at the expense of respect for non-Westerners. Yet there is a mounting accumulation of evidence that all is not well in our impersonal world. Existentialists' prophecies of doom have recently been replaced by hippies' pleas for love, while both Erich Heller and Mircea Eliade have marshalled an impressive weight of evidence that the malaise portrayed in the literature of the West stems from the acosmological impersonalism of Cartesian thought. If, then, theists are to meet or combat the atheisms they have begotten by their surrenders to antithetical modes of thought, it is evident that they must purge themselves of that dehumanizing objectivity that has alienated contemporary man from the earth, from himself, and from his fellow beings. They must become more human than the humanists.

Although some of our theologians appear unaware of the compromises involved in Cartesian thought, in certain areas their "theological sense" has safeguarded them. They recognize, for instance, that the concept of revelation is incompatible with an absolute immanence, and the majority of them react adversely to expressions of a radical existentialism that suggest that one "creates" the meaningful world out of his own substance with the consequence that the past is oppressed by the sheer weight of present responsibility. But the Cartesian view of Reason has always been apologetically enticing and theologians have willy-nilly exploited it to their own detriment. Its fascination is that it compels

---

taken from Van Wing, *Études Bakongo* (Brussels, 1921), pp. 170 ff., as translated by Edwin W. Smith in Smith, ed., *African Ideas of God: A Symposium* (2nd ed. London, Edinburgh House Press, 1950), p. 159.

one to "come in." It conjures up the image of a one-way street. Everybody who thinks must pass from a "descriptive, relational, interpersonal, historical-existential, scriptural" mode of thought and expression to the "definitive, absolute, explanatory, ontological, dogmatic mode."[7] Yet, unlike Descartes, we must ask ourselves whether the building blocks of every system are not cemented by this kind of logic. We have moved beyond his narrow subjectivism because we see knowledge as formed by systems of identification, that is, by groups of interrelated phenomena. Individual letters, for instance, are known as parts of an alphabetic system, just as phonemes, mathematical and chemical signs, and the like are significant as members of sets or series. Without the structures or totalities of microbiology, linguistics, oceanography, and so forth, we cannot locate a definition, a datum, an instrument, or a measurement. In brief, we have replaced subjectivism's unitary "mind" with subjectivity's diversified choice. Wintu cows and Laplander snows are used to illustrate the interdependence of observer and observed, with the result that the hardness of the logical "must" within a system has been tempered by the notion that truth, as Nietzsche saw, is a value. Theologians who are troubled by this suggestion of different systems of truth ought honestly to ask themselves whether, in the light of subjectivism's history, they can afford the price of their Cartesian security.

Throughout this book we shall be constantly returning to the elements of necessity and freedom in truth since modern man's spiritual history is written largely in these terms. On what grounds, we want to know, do we choose our system of values, our truth? Was Kierkegaard right in suggesting a leap, since all of our rationalizing begins from a set *prise de position?* Descartes, in one of his more illuminating suggestions, argued that the idea of God as an infinite or supreme being had to come from God himself since

7. The expressions are John Courtney Murray's in *The Problem of God: Yesterday and Today* (New Haven, Yale University Press, 1964), pp. 49–50.

nothing in our finite experience could suggest such a notion. In other words, the experience of God that grounds his definition is necessarily a rupture of the normal, a theophany or hierophany, perhaps of the kind depicted in the Judaeo–Christian scriptures. It takes something special of this kind to enable us to distinguish "the normal," that is, to see the difference that permits rational choice. Without such an intervention, would we even suspect that the world might be personal?

Certainly other factors than the Cartesian philosophy have been at work in the West undermining Christianity, so that it would be false to conclude from this chapter that Descartes' trend toward anthropology was significantly more than a symptom. On the other hand, as a congenial rational scheme, his philosophy encouraged the attitude it incarnated: a focus on man that, as Nietzsche reminded us, we have not as yet fully exploited. We are still contemplating the values that the Cartesian choices offer us, as if the consequences of some of them in our society have not rationally precluded them. God, in Descartes' system of things, was required for the purposes of human truth. Because He was only a supposition, not a person, He could be dispensed with "on another hypothesis." Man was a mind, a detemporalized, universal Ego. Hegel has depicted how the pretense of this subject to absolute certitude eventually settled him on the level of the empirical Ego, of an animal particularity divorced from spiritual personality. The idea of the world as a connected whole of rigorously logical implications was attacked by empiricists as totally unreal because it contradicted everyday experience. In the following chapter we shall reverse our standpoint in order to consider their hermeneutic of a de-historicized, immediately apprehensible, universal Fact.

FOUR. THE OBSERVATION OF FACTS

–There is an evident absurdity in pretending
to demonstrate a matter of fact, or to prove it
by any arguments *apriori*.
–If we distrust human reason we have now no
other principle to lead us into religion.

HUME, *Dialogues Concerning Natural Religion*

In an age of specialization when it is not inconceivable that
yesterday's truths may metamorphose overnight into today's
errors, we readily find ourselves tongue-tied or paralyzed
by scrupulosity before the delicate task of selecting, collect-
ting, and appraising facts that once appeared perfectly obvious. Selection implies discrimination, collection requires
tools, appraisal entails values. To catalogue or deal with
facts suggests to us, therefore, an increasing complexity of
relationships, unexplored depths of psychology, perhaps
even the permanently inaccessible in the event that we are
trying to resurrect the remotely historical. For the philosopher, the situation is further complicated by the unique
role of history in his dialogue. Parmenides, Duns Scotus,
and Leibniz are cherished for their present contributions
in a way that it would be impossible to think of the discoveries of Harvey or Boyle as challenging a scientist with
alternative programs. For this reason, the philosopher is
necessarily caught up in a constant round of factual reas-
sessments which may strike the outsider as excessively cap-
tious or even inquisitorial. Contemporary philosophers, for
instance, recognize the validity, indeed helpfulness, of the
modes of classification dear to nineteenth-century historians
of philosophy: rationalist, empiricist, idealist, pre-Socratic,

and so forth. But today's thinkers like to shake our complacency by suggesting that something worthwhile has been lost in the process of squeezing people into a mold. What difference would it make to call some of the ancients post-Anaxagorans? Should we not focus more on the discontinuities between Locke, Berkeley, and Hume? Is a dialogue possible when key terms like mind, reason, idea, experience, and human nature derive their meanings from particular contexts that of necessity lose their specific tonality in general categories?

In *A Treatise of Human Nature* and its abridgement, the *Enquiry Concerning Human Understanding,* Hume invited us to consider these terms in a militantly anti-Cartesian context. This does not mean, however, that Hume has nothing positive to contribute to philosophical and religious thought. On the contrary, it is no longer the fashion to regard him unsympathetically as an atheist and metaphysical skeptic. Instead, we are captivated by his uncanny ability to step inside the Cartesian mind in order to exploit the weaknesses of its strength. His exploration of reasoning, notwithstanding the destructive purposes to which it has been put by a host of sensists and empiricists right up to our own day, has practically revolutionized the philosophy of religion by forcing it to sift its criteria of evidence. Other considerations, too, oblige us to peruse his thought. We cannot forget that "An Attempt to Introduce the Experimental Method of Reasoning into Moral Subjects" was the stated purpose of the *Treatise.* By offering a comprehensive vision of man, his world, and God, Hume converted the empirical method into philosophical empiricism. Was his construction an adequate philosophy of natural science? Obviously, Hume's contemporary followers have had to modernize his naïve conception of laboratory techniques. But are they justified in continuing to repeat many of his arguments verbatim? One sometimes has the impression that they have forsaken the spirit of Hume's *Enquiries* for a dogmatic confidence in empiricism. For instance, in certain philosophical enclaves it is a byword that Hume and Kant have shown once and for all how shaky the intellectual grounds are for a belief in a transcendent cause. In fact, some would even maintain that after Hume's *Dialogues Concerning Natural Religion,* religious belief has vanished from circles of the philosophically enlightened. Others have suggested less drastically that the *Dialogues* have hastened the evolution toward a more humane and useful religion, one more consistent with the intellectual implications of a genuinely empirical theory of knowledge. It is, therefore, incumbent upon us to scrutinize the religious intention of these *Dialogues,* as well as the conception of man and the principles of knowledge that undergird them.

Kant was right in stating that Hume attacked Reason, yet he would have been more accurate had he designated the target as Cartesian reasoning. Descartes' key term, intuition, was ambiguous, even though its nuance and his usage favored a stress on the subject's activity. Naturally Hume emphasized impression, since the word conjured up the picture of a mind that is passive in its initial stage. Neither term, of course, connotes primarily the content of knowledge: a fact that is remarkable because it betrays a pyschological preference in Hume no less prominent than that in Descartes. To this important point we must return. Here it is enough to recall that this terminological substitution on the part of Hume epitomized his rejection of the presuppositions without which Descartes' doctrine of intuition was sterile. First, the supposition of isomorphism underlay intuitions, for their psychological impact—clarity and distinctness—resulted from the way things are. Second, God underwrote these intuitions by guaranteeing that their force was due to the way things really are. And third, one can deduce from intuitions (with intuition-like clarity) because of a presumed logical totality. In other words, a more comprehensive intuition that was not explicitly acknowledged as a vision must sustain a system of inferences for, in the last analysis, it is "the light" which allows us to see clearly how things follow. In short, even in Descartes' eminently rational thought the ground of his reasoning was presumed. This, in fact, was the essence of Hume's message: the foundations of reason itself are themselves irrational.

From another viewpoint we can characterize Hume's demurrers as issuing from a flat refusal to acknowledge thought as a metaphorical seeing. In this respect Hume was a literalist. If knowledge is taking a look, then it is restricted within the narrow confines of the immediate present. "Have you ever *seen* nature," Philo importunes Cleanthes at one point in the *Dialogues,*

> in any such situation as resembles the first arrangement of the elements? Have worlds ever been formed *under your eye?* and have you had leisure to *observe* the whole progress of the phenomenon, from the first appearance of order to its final consummation? If you have, then cite your experience, and deliver your theory.[1]

Here is a confidence in visual experience worthy of the most Euclidean-inspired Cartesian.

Yet this passage expresses adequately the essential elements of a philosophical empiricism, which might be expanded as follows. First, observation is less a looking at than a taking in, with the result that experience is described as imposing itself directly upon an organism without the subject's having to organize or constitute it. Second, because visual experience is presumed to be readily testable and universally verifiable, we must suppose that the real world of objective fact exists ready made in an independently "out-there," external order of things. Thus the mind's perceptions (not extractions or abstractions) are verified by looking outside as we do when we assure ourselves that 'the house is white' by personal observation or by applying

1. End of *Dialogue II.* Italics added.

A. J. Ayer's criterion: "Knowing what would be the case if it were true means knowing what observations would verify it."[2] Third, since reasoning is a matter of juggling ideas or hypothesizing, a purely conceptual enterprise, logical rigor is the prerogative of tautologies; empirical certitude belongs to the observed; and a diminishing probability may cling to those statements consistent with, or inferable from, statements of direct observation. Valid inferences, therefore, must comply with two rules: that there are no grounds in any object, considered in itself, which permit us to reason beyond it; and the only objects from which we may draw reasonable conclusions are those of which we have had personal experience.

Historically, we can understand Hume's position in the light of the way that rationalist philosophers spoke of causal inference and of the theological controversy that their talk provoked. We have an example of the former in Locke's celebrated *Essay,* which we know Hume had in mind because he alluded to its illustrations in his discussion "Of Probability" in his first *Enquiry.* Locke had written:

I doubt not but if we could discover the figure, size, texture and motion of the minute constituent parts of any two bodies, we should know without trial several of their operations upon another, as we do now the properties of a square or a triangle. Did we know the mechanical affections of the particles of rhubarb, hemlock, opium, and a man, as a watchmaker does those of a watch, whereby it performs its operations . . . we should be able to tell beforehand that rhubarb will purge, hemlock kill, and opium make a man sleep, as well as a watchmaker can, that a little piece of paper laid on the balance will keep the watch from going,

2. "Logical Positivism: Discussion between Professor Ayer and Father Copleston," in Geddes MacGregor and J. Wesley Robb, eds., *Readings in Religious Philosophy* (Boston, Houghton Mifflin, 1962), p. 345.

till it be removed; or that some small part of it, being rubbed by a file, the machine would quite lose its motions, and the watch go no more.[3]

Hume rightfully insisted that we do not have the kind of knowledge that will justify this apriorism. His objection was that our experience is always of particular instances. Our inferences, however, are based upon generalizations; upon our expectations of what generally, usually, or commonly occurs.

If we are puzzled why theologians were involved in this discussion of probability, we need only recall a remark of Bishop Berkeley's concerning the unprovability of the assumed world of logical implication:

> I do not say *demonstrate,* for all deductions of that kind depend on a supposition that the Author of Nature always operates uniformly, and in a constant observance of those rules we take for principles—which we cannot evidently know.[4]

Here is a clear avowal of the theological presumption of Cartesian reasoning that Hume honestly impugned.

From our privileged vantage point, we can discern how it was that the theology of eighteenth-century England degenerated into a narrow apologetics. Through the influence of Newton's theological lieutenant, Samuel Clarke, religious discussion became for all practical purposes a matter of defending or attacking the philosophical proofs for God, with the result that belief appeared rather as an hypothesis to be proved than as a committed outlook on life. No wonder that Hume insisted that religion was founded on faith, not on reason. This discussion inevitably directed his attention

3. John Locke, *An Essay Concerning Human Understanding,* A. C. Fraser, ed. (Oxford, at the Clarendon Press, 1894), IV, iii, 25.
4. *Principles of Human Knowledge,* Part I, Section 107; Luce-Jessop, ed., 2, 209–11.

to the causal principles upon which the traditional arguments for God were based, and it would seem that his interest in probability and necessary connection dates from the time that he first pondered Berkeley's proofs of the existence and nature of God.[5] Besides, when we recall that Joseph Butler published his famous *Analogy of Religion* at the same time that Berkeley wrote his sustained critique of free-thinking, *Alciphron* (1732), we are led to suspect that Hume's set purpose was to fill the gaping logical hole that Butler acknowledged in his Introduction as "not yet considered."

> When we determine a thing to be probably true (instead of demonstrably true), [or] suppose that an event has or will come to pass, it is from the mind's remarking in it a likeness to some other event, which we have observed has come to pass. And this observation forms, in numberless daily instances, a presumption, opinion, or full conviction, that such an event has or will come to pass. But it is not my design to enquire further into the nature, the foundation, and measure of probability; or whence it proceeds that *likeness* should beget presumption, opinion, and full conviction, which the human mind is formed to receive from it, and which it does not necessarily produce in every one; or to guard against the error to which reasoning from analogy is liable. This belongs to the subject of logic, and is a part of that subject which has not yet been thoroughly considered.[6]

Considering his times, we can esteem Bishop Butler's prudence in refusing to discuss the nature and foundation of probability even though this was the crucial problem.

5. Charles W. Hendel, Jr., *Studies in the Philosophy of David Hume* (Princeton, N.J., Princeton University Press, 1925), p. 189.
6. Joseph Butler, *The Analogy of Religion* (New York, Bell & Daldy 1868), p. 74.

It would take a mind of Nietzsche's fiber to flush out the real issues and to stalk the "godless anti-metaphysicians" in a promethean effort to make them choose for or against truth. Does not all thought, he asked, suppose the existence of truth, that is, of some kind of system and therefore God? But Nietzsche had the advantage of post-Hegelian hindsight so that his reflections could benefit from Hume's search for a satisfactory alternative to the Cartesian reliance upon a divine guarantee. The irony of Hume's position, I would suggest, is that many of his followers have extracted the sensist element of his thought in order to provide this alternative to the Cartesian way. His own thought, however, veered elsewhere. Acting upon Butler's suggestion, Hume seems to have looked for a solution in the direction of man's imagination and his "natural beliefs."

Take for example the statement of the *Treatise* that is frequently cited by contemporary empiricists.

> There is a direct and total opposition between our reason and our senses, or more properly speaking, between those conclusions we form from cause and effect, and those that persuade us of the continued and independent existence of body. When we reason from cause and effect, we conclude, that neither colour, sound, taste, nor smell have a continued and independent existence. When we exclude these sensible qualities there remains nothing in the universe, which has such an existence.[7]

Surely the point of this passage, although it was made within the language and the purview of the technical philosophy of the day, expresses the conviction that underlay Hume's philosophical activity: that philosophers have been subverters of common sense. The critique of the ancient and modern philosophy in the *Treatise* makes the point more

7. Hume, *A Treatise of Human Nature*, L. A. Selby-Bigge, ed. (Oxford, at the Clarendon Press, 1955), p. 231.

tellingly. The ancients exploited a natural belief in the permanence of objects that leads one to consider sensations as qualities of an independent substance. On the other hand, the moderns centered on a natural belief in the dynamic interdependence of events that leads one to regard sensations as subjective states, products of psychophysical reactions. Presumably one can try, as Descartes did, to reconcile these beliefs theoretically. But his construction relied on the gratuitous assumption of isomorphism. Hence it never dawned on him to resolve this dilemma by taking philosophical principles for what they really are, that is, as tools of organization for practical ends.

It is true that Hume argued his point with all the resources of an empirical theory of knowledge. Because, he contended, the vast majority of our ideas lack immediate entrance into the world of fact, they are "copies" that only with great difficulty can be traced to their originating impressions. Had he been strictly logical, he probably should have moved in a Kantian direction and referred to these ideas as *bliks* (in Richard Hare's jargon), for they are the constructs that allow us to perceive the world in a certain way. But *bliks* as filters are incontestable, as Kant showed. Hence it is not surprising, given Hume's passion for verification, that he eschewed talk about attitudes in his hermeneutic of the observed fact. Unlike his contemporary followers, he had no need to foist upon us the belief that everything depends upon whim. Perhaps he realized that if one way of seeing the world—theistically or atheistically— is as good as another, it is impossible to engage in meaningful debate.

In summary, we might characterize the difference in emphasis between Hume and contemporary empiricists as follows. First, they have heightened the mind-world dichotomy by extricating the decisive argument of the *Dialogues,* part of which was cited at the beginning of this chapter, from its polemical setting.

I shall begin with observing, that there is an evident absurdity in pretending to demonstrate a matter of fact, or to prove it by an argument *apriori*. Nothing is demonstrable, unless the contrary implies a contradiction. Nothing, that is distinctly conceivable, implies a contradiction. Whatever we conceive as existent, we can also conceive as non-existent. There is no being, therefore, whose non-existence implies a contradiction. Consequently there is no being, whose existence is demonstrable. I propose this argument as entirely decisive, and am willing to rest the whole controversy upon it.[8]

Certainly if we take the key terms of this argument as Hume understood them: observe, demonstrate, fact, and existence, it is evident that we cannot derive ideal necessity from real contingency. Unfortunately, Hume did not elaborate upon his equating of conceivability with imaginability: a move that prepared Kant's refutation of the "ontological argument" and prompted Gilbert Ryle's remark that "conceptual considerations" cannot deliver positive "existence conclusions."[9]

Second, they have taken Hume's description of the mind as the "faculty of compounding, transposing, augmenting, or diminishing the materials afforded us by the sense and experience"[10] to show that its implication has been expressed by that group of philosophers, including James, Dewey, Russell, and Ryle, who maintain that mind is only a relation or function. Therefore, there is "no other principle to lead us into religion."

Third, a major point of difference between Hume and our contemporaries is that the latter have been embarrassed

8. *Dialogue IX.*

9. See the final discussion in D. F. Pears, ed., *The Nature of Metaphysics* (London, Macmillan, 1957), pp. 148–50.

10. *An Enquiry Concerning Human Understanding*, Section II; Selby-Bigge ed., p. 19.

by a view of man or his mind that has minimized human creativity. As a consequence of Hume's naïve understanding of scientific method, he fostered the delusion that Newton's shibboleth, "Hypotheses non fingo," should be translated "I feign no hypotheses." The word "hypothesis" is thus saddled with a pejorative connotation, as in the case of the statement that evolution is "only a hypothesis," or "It's only a hypothesis that smoking causes lung cancer." In other words, the inventive aspect of scientific knowledge was swallowed in the observational. We are to imagine the scientist as testing his theories by comparing them with "naked facts," as if the sophisticated gadgets of our laboratories were not instruments in the process of "seeing as."[11] Today we know that it is impossible to envisage scientific inquiry as to this kind of cold, dispassionate enterprise, bleached of imaginative qualities. By nature it is a promotion of natural knowledge (in a true sense, therefore, a passionate undertaking), in which one interrogates "Nature" with an end in view, confident that "She" will respond in accord with his anticipations. Observation, in other words, is an experience, not just an act. It is governed by intentionality since it is, literally, an *ob-servare:* a preservation *for the sake of,* or a keeping hold of something *on account of.*

In conclusion, we might note the obvious discrepancy for contemporary empiricists who insist upon the separation of theory from fact and yet are torn by its consequences in the realm of theory. "What seems to me clear," Michael Scriven has confessed, "is that even the least theoretical approach is absolutely committed to the use of concepts which are quite definitely not abbreviations for observation-

11. See: Jerome S. Bruner, Jacqueline J. Goodnow, George A. Austin, *A Study of Thinking* (New York, Science Editions, Inc., 1962). Eugene T. Gendlin, *Experiencing and the Creation of Meaning: A Philosophical and Psychological Approach to the Subjective* (Glencoe, The Free Press, 1962). Norwood Russell Hanson, *Patterns of Discovery: An Inquiry into the Conceptual Foundations of Science* (Cambridge, at the University Press, 1961).

language complexes, i.e. no translation rules are available."[12] If, notwithstanding empiricist theory, we must admit that there can be partial mappings of one language upon another, or modes of analogy between theory and fact, what is to prevent us from breaking even farther out of empiricism? Does not this correlation compel us to surrender the narrow anthropology underlying the theory for a view of man and his mind that is really metaphysical, one, that is, which ultimately makes room for theology within the scope of the rational?

> It is perfectly clear that existential hypotheses . . . cannot be logically translated into statements about evidential data . . . Positivistic–phenomenalistic attempts at "reduction" of these concepts must now be regarded as complete failures. According to the network analysis of scientific concepts and laws, the verifying evidence is to be viewed as causally related to the evidenced "theoretical" entities. If this be metaphysics, make the most of it.[13]

The network theory to which Herbert Feigl here refers is an allusion to the Kantian mentality of the early Wittgenstein. It has the peculiarity that even though our propositions are assertions about the net and never about what the net "describes," nevertheless, "Through their entire logical apparatus the laws of physics still speak about the objects of the world."[14] On the face of it, this looks like an act of

12. "Definitions, Explanations, and Theories," in *Minnesota Studies in the Philosophy of Science* (Minneapolis, University of Minnesota Press, 1958), 2, 192.

13. H. Feigl, "Philosophy of Science of Logical Empiricism," in *Minnesota Studies, 1*, 17. See also Robert Oppenheimer, "The Growth of Science and the Structure of Culture: Comments on Dr. Frank's Paper," in Gerald Holton, ed., *Science and the Modern Mind: A Symposium* (Boston, Beacon Press, 1958); and Ernest Nagel, *The Structure of Science: Problems in the Logic of Scientific Explanation* (New York, Harcourt, Brace & World, 1961).

14. L. Wittgenstein, *Tractatus Logico-Philosophicus*, 6.3431.

faith not unworthy of Descartes.[15] Logically, it would appear more honest to deny this faith and to subscribe to Hobbes' thesis of conventionalism, that reasoning is merely a stringing together of names by the word "is," so that we can draw no conclusions about the real natures of things. But miraculously, this thesis has been resurrected by the early Wittgenstein and others, even though John Stuart Mill brilliantly refuted it with his theory of connotation. Apparently we must still live with the assertion that regularity, possibility, and necessity are concepts of logic which are irrelevant to contingent, utterly independent states of affairs.[16]

15. In one of our popular magazines (*Time*, July 6, 1962) a scientist has made this act of faith explicit.

Re. the article on faith and the scientist [June 29]: there is an unwarranted assumption that science deals in faithless fact and that religion traffics in factless faith. The quote from Dr. Van Ness sums it up perfectly: "Any time religious *beliefs* come into conflict with the things we *learn* about the world, we must modify the beliefs." Any number of the scientific concepts we accept today may be simply convenient schemata that impose order upon the experiences we have collected so far. They may have little or no relation to "reality."

The suspicion has been growing among many scholars during the past few decades that we are not so much "discovering" our scientific theories as we are "inventing" them. A theory is thus neither true nor false; it simply works or it doesn't. Now it is true that many scientists (including myself) *believe* that their theories closely approximate or correspond to "reality," but this is an act of faith, for no "proof" can be adduced for or against it. Scientific beliefs can conflict with religious beliefs, but the large number of modified or even discarded scientific theories should serve as a useful warning relating to Dr. Van Ness' pronouncement. We should be very careful about junking our deep, personal religious committals because of certain presently held schemes that we are attempting to apply to the natural world, however useful they may be at the moment. Philosophically, this is an odd way of talking, one that should make us wary of its presuppositions and anxious to rescue its author from his restricted notion of truth. Although he juxtaposes *true* and *useful,* he intimates that both are value concepts.

16. Wittgenstein, *Tractatus*, 6.3, 6.375, 2.061–2.062. The logical inconsistency concerning 'contingent' and 'necessary' has been pointed out by Martha and William Kneale in their book, *The Development of Logic* (Oxford, at the Clarendon Press, 1962), esp. pp. 629 ff.

By noting a difference of emphasis between Hume and his contemporary followers, we have actually agreed that there is textual evidence in Hume for present-day developments. Yet it is by no means obvious that he would approve a rendition of his thought that chooses to ignore the implications of his talk about the imagination, his interest in association and "custom," and, in his moral philosophy, sentiment and taste. Such notions may be oddities in an intellectualist style of thought, but it is patent that Hume could not dispense with them if he wanted to attack reason, and a fortiori if he wanted to discuss religion. Consequently, if we focus his empiricist theory of knowledge in a proper historical perspective, and interpret the passages culled by contemporary empiricists as serving a polemical purpose, we begin to appreciate the nature of his hostility to traditional metaphysics. If reasoning requires a context or structure, if in reality the process of deductive inference is set in motion by a holistic vision or a supposed totality, we must admit that the ground of reasoning is nonrational, even, of course, if we are prepared to agree that the inaugurating vision "becomes rational" in the course of its explication. Now, since the traditional arguments for God were formed out of the vision or the structure of reasoning, it is clear why Hume's assault on this ground of metaphysics was simultaneously an incursion into theology.

We can, indeed, arrest Hume in his negative phase, as contemporary empiricists are wont to do—"Our holy religion is founded on *faith*, not on reason"—from which we are supposed to conclude that because Hume discerned that religion was supposed by, and thus could not be established by, Cartesian reasoning, he presumed that it could in no way be grounded at all. But if that were his persuasion, why did he mention "natural beliefs"? Why in the *Treatise*, as he grappled with Bishop Butler's difficulty, did he define imagination as the faculty at work whenever belief, and not mere feigning, is in possession of the mind? Imagination in this sense, we should note, is said to be operative only when principles that are permanent, irresistible, and universal are in control, for belief, as a basic component of human nature, is not subject to the individual's arbitrary choice. These would seem, then, to be the fruitful Humean suggestions that awakened Kant from his "dogmatic slumber." They were suggestions that, for one reason or another, lay dormant in Hume, perhaps because of a too exalted notion of science and the demands of its empiricist concept of knowledge. Kant, regrettably, did not do much better with them. The schematizing operation of the Transcendental Imagination, which was central to his blueprint, was sketched in tantalizingly meager strokes. Undeniably, he was too much the intellectualist in his brilliant synthesis of Cartesian and Humean principles to accomplish more than a transposition of the difficulty. (The imagination, we might recall, has traditionally been described as a bodily faculty that somehow bridges sense and intellect. Understandably, it is ignored by disincarnating intellectualist philosophies that sacrifice man to mind.)

God, both of these men affirmed, somehow belongs to the experience of man. The divine is in a fashion rooted in habits of living that cannot be rationally articulated to everyone's satisfaction. Perhaps we can share to a degree the frustration of Hume and Kant when we read accounts of the religions of the world and wonder how these oft-competing presentations might be grounded. Eventually we may say "in faith," but we tend to shy away from this reply for fear that we might impress others as anti-intellectual. Undoubtedly that was the way it impressed Hume and Kant, and so it will be until someone arrives on the scene who can, by a thorough-going exploration of human nature, disabuse all philosophers of preconceived, confining models of rationality.

In a sense all Christians must agree with Hume. Their "holy religion is founded on *faith,* not on reason" for no system of metaphysics can establish it. Yet a glance at the religions of the world ought to convince the Christian of the import of that qualification. In fact, Hume's hints regarding the imagination and his tentative program of an exploration of natural beliefs seem to confirm the truth developed by all traditional arguments for God since the time of Augustine: that built into the dialectic or structure of the human mode of being-in-the-world (i.e. thought) is the possibility of a revealed religion.

Part of the inspiration of this chapter has been my conviction that we will for a long time, if not always, rely on Hume-inspired reflections in order to curb the dogmatic pretensions of reason. If we must live in the West with two conflicting cultures, should we not anticipate at least a minimum of two conflicting philosophies? As long as the influence of Descartes continues to make itself felt in Western thought, we will be tempted to "excarnate" ourselves: to impoverish the temporalizing, diversifying body in order to enrich a monopolizing, uniquely functioning mind. Both Hume and Kant, I have suggested, discerned this temptation, although they were too much of their times to escape it.

Moreover, because of the prominence of empiricist thought in the West, I have also been concerned to present as clearly as possible the nature of empiricist reflection so that our theologians might be fully aware of their commitments when they adapt in part or wholly adopt this philosophical outlook. For as a reflection, empiricism is merely an articulation of one's lived experience of man and world, with or without God. Reflection, in other words, brings out and sets before us the components of our experience. And so, when we are invited to see ourselves as immersed in a natural, scientific world of faithless fact in which a factless faith does not reach the surface of rational reflection, we have every right to suppose that notwithstanding a great deal of lip service paid to religion, God cannot really constitute an element of experience. Ironically, the Humean–

Kantian premises, as in the thought of Rudolf Otto, may have served to extol the gratuity of grace. But in reality, by a theory of knowledge that takes religion outside the rules of rational confirmability, empiricists have succeeded in inculcating an atheistic experience. Nietzsche was not wrong in testifying to a despiritualizing influence in Western culture.

It is not to our purpose to discuss the much-heralded remedy for our present religious crisis, that, namely, of secularizing theology and enhancing its scientific prestige by trying to fit it within the canons of empiricist thought. Nor is it germane to consider the consequent linguistic problem, even though a number of theologians would have us believe that the current lack of religious communication is due entirely to the language and/or meanings of Christian dogma and theology. At bottom, we lack the studies in depth of religious attrition that might substantiate the virtues of these panaceas. Until that time, however, we must distinguish intellectually how much of our popular jeremiads and *Honest to God's* is a product of pastoral frustrations, supplemented by browsings in Nietzsche and Bonhoeffer, and how much is a reliable index of a widespread loss of faith as opposed to a change in the forms of faith.

Assuredly it is difficult to impress upon the philosophically innocent theologian his predicament when he surmises that his relevance is dependent upon his theologizing from a position where "world" is defined as composed of hard or neutral "facts" that, unlike so-called religious data, are incontrovertible precisely because they require no privileged access. For how does the theist extricate his "religious meaning" from this presumed common store of experience? Or how does he show that this meaning is more humanly significant than a purely secular interpretation of the "same" world? Religion, then, is a matter of attitude, the product, perhaps, of educational indoctrination, and really an obstacle to seeing the world neutrally. The difference, obviously, between debating the religious problems of modern technocracy on this terrain and on the grounds that the facts of religion involve the response of the whole man to his estimate of the reality of things is that the theologian has surrendered the world to the empiricist. How does he then talk sensibly about creation or incarnation? His attitude is a take-it-or-leave-it affair; his religious commitment can be adequately expressed in the statement: "I am partial to God-talk."

Although philosophical empiricism has augmented the theological problems of modern technocracy, there are other, perhaps more subtly psychological, factors involved in the religious challenge of this modern mentality. Technocracy offers us a mode of thinking about ourselves and the world that is indifferent to religious understanding. Judaism and Christianity, for instance, are not unlike the religions of the Dinka, Navahoes, Aztecs, or Hurons in that they tell us who man is. They provide accounts which inform a people (mankind) of their origins, their world-situation (historical and geographical position), and their destiny. Thus *homo religiosus* is at home in the world, even though his encounters with the Sacred or the Transcendent make him conscious of his dependence and finitude. The general practice of the churches of the West has deepened this passive attitude on the part of their adherents. The initiated have more frequently been acknowledged as hearers or the faithful than as communicants. But with the ascendancy of modern science creativity has come to the fore; the sense of dependency has been weakened by the recession of the old limitations of thought; a frightening alienation has developed, since we tend to look upon ourselves as insignificant molecules or specks of cosmic dust, tossed about by nature's blind forces, and destined to have our most noteworthy achievements demolished if somebody thoughtlessly pulls the wrong switch. No wonder existentialists, having

diagnosed our anxiety, have offered prognoses and prescriptions for our sickness unto death and meaninglessness.
Moreover, the scientific method, which because of its technological success has impressed many thinkers as the only fruitful approach to reality, can operate against theological thought. For the sake of clarity, we might oversimplify by distinguishing two phases of scientific procedure: the first, hypothesis, consists in interrogating as partisan and participant. The scientist has his *parti pris*, and so constrains the world to deliver his meanings. In this sense he is a creator of meaning. The second phase is that of verification: devising different kinds of experiment or test for the meaning he has found. Scientific knowledge, therefore, is characteristically human: the project of human initiative, progressively confirmed or disconfirmed, focused on the behavior and results of immediate, external "facts," and scrapped or revised under the pressure of corroborative or discordant data. In comparison to this pursuit that suggests the excitement of novelty and the unexpected, theology has been made into the image of a divine *fiat*, that is, of any authoritative declaration of the Word of God. Falsely, no doubt, it has become identified with its caricature: namely, that eternal truths preclude persistent discovery, that once-and-for-all-events gainsay new insights and evolving conditions, and that absolute standards of right and wrong forbid reappraisals.

In addition to the obvious remedy of repairing their image, to the extent, at least, of suggesting that theological truth develops within the community of the faithful under the guidance of the Spirit, some theologians have attempted to find a point of insertion for their reflection as it were within, not along side of, scientific method. They have tried to avoid the encumbrances of the old natural theology as well as the obstacles of empiricism by looking to the first, the interrogating, stage of scientific hypothesis. Could there be any participation at all, any dialogue with or in the world, were one not convinced that the whole enterprise is worthwhile? Thus, instead of looking to religion or theology for that type of explanation which we might expect from natural science or history, we more properly locate it as a value or, correctly understood, as an attitude that conditions our subsequently developed modes of patterning the world but which, unlike these modes, offers an overriding meaning or purpose to life. Religion belongs, then, to empirical thought as its horizon. In this way the operational or functional aspects of knowledge are accorded their just place without usurping the field of human truth.

Perhaps this point and some of its ramifications can be illustrated by an example from another discipline. At the present time how history is to be defined is still a moot subject. Invariably the controversies of the past have been controlled by philosophical premises—witness the thought of Hegel, Ranke, Droysen, and Dilthey—which should alert us to the play of values in a purportedly factual study. Edward Carr has vividly described the situation: the fish the historian catches depends partly upon chance, but mainly upon the part of the ocean he chooses to fish and the kind of gear he selects, both of which are determined by the kind of fish he wants to catch.[17] There are fish to be caught, and, at this point the metaphor breaks down, we must suppose that one is also convinced that fishing is worthwhile. It is, in fact, not a sport at all but something he must do if he is to be an intelligent, integral man. Ultimately, history falls back upon an anthropology that continues to be a theological question.

The alternative to this view is, of course, the empiricist perspective, represented by Carl Hempel and others who are interested in the logic of historical narration and the

17. *What Is History?* (New York, Knopf, 1963).

nature of covering laws.[18] Because empiricism places a
premium on the immediate present as the proper datum of
science, there is a danger that one's descriptions of the past
may be punctuated by "primitive," "antiquarian," "mythological," and similarly pejorative expressions that convey
the impression that the past is actually of secondary import to scientific man. History, accordingly, is apt to
be defined as a sort of amassing of facts, interesting for those
who like that kind of collecting, but not essential to man's
self-revelation. Opponents of this view have deplored it as
the terror of historicism because it cuts contemporary man
off from his roots. It exploits the "objective" methods of
the natural sciences to the point that the web is broken, so
that history, as an *histos* or tissue of relations which knits
elements of tradition together into a revealing structure
for contemporary man, falls apart. Our meaninglessness and
religious rootlessness can be traced to our loss of culture,
to the disappearance of that shared history which permits
all of us to discourse because we are situated both temporally
and locally in a common cosmos, an ordered system in which
we know our way about.

Paradoxical as it may seem, it is not strange that existentialists and theologians should join forces against an
empiricist concept of history. For is not the real issue for
both groups the same? When man has severed the cultural
ties that bind him to his fellow man and the world, his
liberty is in jeopardy. The pseudo-tranquility of a determinism unrelieved by any rupture from without rapidly
degenerates into chaos as communications break down.
Everyone and everything loom up before him as an hostile
"other," and the situation of dialogue that religion needs
in order to exist has been destroyed. No wonder that Hegel

18. Papers arguing both points of view can be found in *Philosophy and
History: A Symposium*, Sidney Hook, ed. (New York, NYU Press, 1963).

sought to overcome the Humean–Kantian "scientific" thought through a dialectic of freedom.

When we rethink Hume's *Dialogues* from the standpoint of freedom, we can see that he has raised a profound, and therefore perennial, question of religious psychology. If, as Hume saw, one's practical conduct is sufficient to dissipate a philosophical solipsism or other form of skepticism about the world, why is it that religious practice is not an equally effective antidote to religious skepticism? We are caught in a crevasse between theory and practice. If, on the one hand, virtue is not knowledge, and, on the other, religious-appearing conduct is no guarantee of genuine commitment, then the question is imperative: What is the relationship of theory or rational reflection to religious life and conviction?

It is clear that the principles of Hume's philosophy of observation will not permit us to discuss this question of realization intelligently. However vague the terms, we cannot do without notions like intention, insight, or conviction when we try to mark the difference between pure theory and actualization. A univocally functioning Cartesian Reason, with its correlatively absolute concepts of proof, evidence, interpretation, and the like, led inevitably into Hume's epistemology, in which the dynamism of lived experiencing broke down into a dichotomy between a neutral empirical world that justified neither a theistic nor an atheistic outlook and one's gratuitously assumed attitude toward life. It is difficult, indeed, to imagine how theologians could ever have accepted this radical separation of knowing and understanding from believing and doing without questioning their function as teachers and preachers. Why is it that so much of the process of conduct formation is devoted to teaching principles and doctrines, to teaching by example, even coming to know another in order to be drawn to virtue through love? Thus for us to describe the religion of the Nuer, the Aruak, the Bakuena, or the Hebrews as an attitude in the empiricist sense is seriously misleading and in the long run conducive, as Santayana shrewdly observed concerning William James' approach to religion, to a disintegration of the idea of truth, to a recommendation of belief without reason, and to an encouragement of superstition. One could not be an Israelite, that is, share that form of life and world of signification, unless he acknowledged God's "works" and believed. Thus, in a context in which belief is in reality a whole way of life, it is clearly meaningless to try to point out a hypothetically neutral empirical fact.

"I can only presume to speak for a majority," Herbert Read has alleged,

who regard this divided and tragic world we live in as devoid of any compelling image of reconciliation; therefore absurd. I think I still speak for a majority when I further assume that no compelling image of reconciliation is found in existing religions; or, if it does exist there, is disturbed by dogma and conventional behavior—by what Kierkegaard in his righteous zeal called an "impudent indecency."[19]

This need for reconciliation led Hegel to attack the subjective and objective hermeneutics upon which the Kantian science of his day was based. There was, accordingly, a theological concern behind the synthesis around Life in his early Jena system, as well as in his later synthesis around Spirit. Man is a unit; the thrust of his rationality is a drive toward unification. He cannot live without attempting to reconcile inner with outer, to compose subjective and objective contradictions, to clarify ambiguities by discovering or introducing harmonizing principles. Hegel's project, which we shall consider in part in the following chapter, was thus

19. *The Form of Things Unknown* (New York, Horizon Press, 1960), p. 176.

carefully aimed at bringing us back to the traditional stream of philosophy, namely, to a deeper examination of reflective thought that would free it from the prison of intellectualism. Before proceeding, we might remind ourselves that these analytical chapters on Saint Anselm, Descartes, and Hume have been intended to prelude the more speculative chapters to follow. Having familiarized ourselves with the major trends or convergence of thought in the traditional philosophy of religion, we are ready to explore the possibilities opened up to us by the contemporary world.

FIVE. THE PARADOX OF THOUGHT

> As man, religion is essential to him, and is not
> a feeling foreign to his nature. Yet the essen-
> tial question is the relation of religion to his
> general theory of the universe, and it is with
> this that philosophical knowledge connects
> itself, and upon which it essentially works.
>
> HEGEL, *Lectures on the Philosophy of Re-
> ligion*

Great philosophical minds have always succeeded in provok-
ing controversy, but few philosophers have so consistently
stirred elemental passions as Hegel. In Europe his influence
continues unparalleled. He is, as Maurice Merleau-Ponty
declared, the fountainhead of all the interesting philosophical currents of the last century: Marxism, Nietzsche, phenomenology, German existentialism, and psychoanalysis.[1]
Our tentative explorations of the irrational in order to
integrate it into a broader concept of reason draw their
inspiration from him. To this continental respect, the philosophical opinion of Britain and the United States presents
a sharp contrast. Many of the present-day older generation
philosophers rebelled against the Hegelianism they had
learned from F. H. Bradley, so that with a few notable ex-
ceptions the younger generation has been reared in indifference to, if not antipathy toward, Hegel's thought. As a
consequence, these philosophers have not been motivated
to consult up-to-date European scholarship and are apt to
rely for their scattered information on our pitiful supply of

1. "L'existentialisme chez Hegel," in *Sens et Non-sens* (Paris, Nagel,
1948), p. 125.

English works. It is a blight upon the scholarship of the English-speaking world that there has been no intense pressure exerted for a first-rate work that takes one beyond the introductory stage; and it is unflattering to our critical judgment that a tendentious book based on extensive ignorance and misconception like *The Open Society and Its Enemies* should have been so favorably received by us and frequently reprinted.[2]

This rather harsh judgment might serve as a warning to those theologians who feel that to be *au courant* one must condemn metaphysics *in globo* and on occasion refer to Hegel as the high priest of aprioristic philosophical triumphalism. But it will not do to retain a memory-image of Hegel gathered from the philosophers of religion and "natural theologians" of the early years of this century. Instead, we ought to bear in mind that the gist of Hegel's thought was to repair that dialectical link between believing and thinking which had been weakened during the deistic controversy and left in ruins by the "scientific" labors of Hume and Kant. In a word, he is the philosopher of reconciliation, and so a man with a message for contemporary theologians.

It is generally admitted that Hegel's personal religious convictions are indecipherable, and the division of Hegelians into factions of the conservative, religious-oriented Right and of the radical, atheistically inclined Left indicates that the problem is not to be resolved by a simple marshaling of texts. We know, too, that the censuring of Fichte and other professors by an overzealous government had its sobering impact on everybody with liberal inclinations. For this reason also, Hegel, as one of his critics has

2. Perhaps Karl Popper's readers believe it worthwhile to read about a man who "had not even talent." See T. M. Knox's review article, "Hegel in English-speaking Countries since 1919," *Hegel-Studien, 1* (1961), 316.

remarked, prudently departed for the grave with his secret intact.[3] Not so, says Walter Kaufmann, whose vigorous dissent deserves mention because of the availability of his writings to American readers.[4] For years Kaufmann has been conducting a campaign to persuade us that Hegel never expected salvation from Christianity. As early as 1795, when he published his *Life of Jesus*, Hegel, we are to believe, was convinced once and for all that man could not be restored to harmony through religion. Ironically, Kaufmann would have us take the youth for the man. Instead of having us read the juvenilia in the spirit of Fichte's *Essay Toward a Critique of All Revelation* (1792) or Kant's *Religion Within the Limits of Reason Alone* (1793), Kaufmann has proposed that we should dismiss all of Hegel's subsequent reflections on religion as aberrant. Perversely, Hegel deteriorated interiorly in inverse proportion to his soaring philosophical reputation, for Kaufmann has claimed that the later obscurity and basic flaws that he has detected in Hegel's "mature" thought are traceable directly to "the traditionalist effort to discover the epitome of reason in his Christian

3. Franz Grégoire, *Étude hégéliennes: les points capitaux du système* (Louvain, Nauwelaerts, 1958), p. 216. There exists a wealth of literature for both sides. J. MacBride Sterrett, *Studies in Hegel's Philosophy of Religion* (New York, 1890), is typical of the older group who thought of Hegel as radically and throughout a theologian. Two of the better known antitheological treatises are those of Alexandre Kojève, *Introduction à la lecture de Hegel: leçons sur la Phénoménologie de l'esprit* (3rd ed. Paris, Gallimard, 1947), and G. Lukács, *Der junge Hegel, Über die Beziehungen von Dialektik und Ökonomie* (Zürich-Wien, 1948), which were written in opposition to the views of Theodor L. Häring's monumental work, *Hegel, sein Wollen und sein Werk* (2 vols. Leipzig, Teubner, 1929, 1938) (reprinted by the Scientia Verlag Aalen, 1963), and to restore the balance which they felt had been upset by an overenthusiastic reception of Nohl's edition of the so-called *Early Theological Writings*.

4. His most recent work—a disappointment—is *Hegel: Reinterpretation, Texts, Commentary* (New York, Doubleday, 1965), which merely repeats (pp. 62–63) the views on religion expressed in his earlier writings.

heritage and to find his own philosophy implicit in the ancient dogmas."[5]

Apart from the suspect disingenuousness of this interpretation, is it not more natural to suppose that as Hegel grew in stature his philosophy became more subtly anti-Kantian? Is not a measure of *raffinement* or preciousness inevitable when one trains his sights on an entrenched orthodoxy?

> We cannot know God as object, or get a real knowledge of him, and the main thing, what we are really concerned about, is merely the subjective manner of knowing him and our subjective religious condition. We may recognize this standpoint as described in what has just been said. It is the standpoint of the age . . .[6]

The attacking philosopher is always in the position of one charging up a slippery slope. As one who writes for his colleagues, he cannot eschew a traditional vocabulary. Yet as a critic of the establishment who is anxious to introduce his own outlook, he is forced to give this vocabulary a personal twist. The Heideggerian corpus, for which Kaufmann has reserved some of his choicest obloquy, suffers from the same disadvantage. Unfortunately, the dichotomies of common sense favor the clearcut subject–object talk of Descartes, Hume, and Kant, in comparison with which the tortured languages of Hegel and Heidegger smack of barbarism and obscurantism.

Moreover, one manifests little understanding of the Hegelian maneuver by trying to create the impression that Hegel's sustained religious preoccupation was only the

5. "Hegel: Contribution and Calamity," *From Shakespeare to Existentialism: Studies in Poetry, Religion and Philosophy* (Boston, Beacon Press, 1959), pp. 158 ff.

6. *Lectures on the Philosophy of Religion, Together with a Work on the Proofs of the Existence of God*, Eng. trans. from the second German edition (Marheineke) Rev. E. B. Speirs and J. Burdon Sanderson (London, Routledge & Kegan Paul, 1962) (reprinted), 2, 331. In German, *Sämtliche Werke* (Jubiläumsausgabe) (Stuttgart, Frohmann Verlag, 1959), *16*, 194.

whim of old age. As we know, the empiricist epistemology of Kant had relegated God to faith. From Hegel's standpoint, this artificial divorce of the *Verstand* from the *Vernunft* had bequeathed to philosophy an area of pure understanding operating on sense data, and to theology the domain of speculatively unverifiable postulates. Because Hegel found it contradictory to discourse about a Supreme Lawgiver who is not Ultimate Truth, or to believe in a God of revelation who has not revealed Himself to man's intelligence, he concentrated on redefining philosophical knowledge in such a way that it would harmonize the discord of reason and religion: "to show how we know this latter [religion] to be in all its manifold forms necessary, and to rediscover in revealed religion the truth and the Idea."[7] And so, rather than think of the young Hegel as having been visited by mystic promptings, and of his mature philosophy as a form of deviationism, we must credit him with the awareness that in the existential order a Christian's description of knowledge is unavoidably a comment on faith. Hegel, in other words, had to talk about religion because he wanted to discuss knowledge, and that not simply for the reason that he was busy pursuing the Kantian quarry. If, of course, Professor Kaufmann were correct, Hegel's work would have been greatly simplified. The reconciliation of religion and knowledge would have been accomplished through reduction. In that event, dialectical difficulties would have disappeared because "otherness" would have been suppressed, and we would have to interpret seemingly forthright statements as pieces of pious edification:

> The aim of philosophy is to know the truth, to know God, for He is the absolute truth, inasmuch as nothing else is worth troubling about save God and the unfolding of God's nature . . . Philosophy, which is the-

7. *Lectures on the Philosophy of Religion, 3,* 151; *SW, 16,* 355.

ology, is solely concerned with showing the rationality of religion.[8]

If philosophy is theology, it is only because the aim of philosophical or reflective knowledge is to show how religion, confined by the Kantians within the scope of practical reason, is related to one's "general theory of the universe," that is, to the creations of his speculative reason. This point should be emphasized not only because it is important for our grasp of the intent of Hegel's work but also because we can avoid endless disputes with those philosophers who justifiably resent the insinuation that Hegel was interested exclusively in religious questions. In the previous chapters we have unfolded the ideas of understanding which he could not accept. Starting from Descartes' dichotomy of subject and object, the philosophers of the rationalist tradition developed the "flint" notion of Reason, which enabled them to display reasoning as a mathematical, inductive–deductive process. Two consequences of importance followed: a risk of making God totally immanent and a universe of total implication, in which the order and connection of things stood in one-to-one correspondence with the order and connection of ideas. Hume attacked both this idea of Reason and its world of entailments by playing up the opposition of reason to sense. Kant, whom Hölderlin described to his brother as the "Moses of our nation who leads it out of the Egyptian somnolence into the free, lonely desert of his speculation and brings the energizing law from the holy mountain,"[9] attempted to synthesize these traditions by a crucial distinction of the mind's structures. The Categories and Concepts of the Understanding *(Verstand)*

8. Ibid., 148; *SW, 16,* 352–53. I have argued some of these points more extensively and tried to show that some of the theologians' fears of Hegel are due to his unregenerate Kantianism in "Hegel as Philosopher of Religion," *The Journal of Religion, 46* (1966), 9–23.

9. Cited by Richard Kroner, *Von Kant Bis Hegel* (2nd ed. Tübingen, J. C. B. Mohr, 1961), 2 vols. in 1, p. 3 n. 2.

functioned exclusively as unifiers of empirical data, that is, of perceived phenomena, whereas Reason *(Vernunft)* operated with nonempirical, umbrella-like ideas or ideals—God, Soul, and World—which were necessary unifying schemes in the overall process of comprehension. The upshot of this analysis was a metaphysics of finitude that left one ultimately in an unbridgeable problem of the noumenon. How can we relate man's sense-dependent knowledge and the postulates of reason required for organizing it to the extramental limiting concept of the thing-in-itself? With the hope of solving this problem Kant had turned to an investigation of the practical reason. But there too he found himself in a dilemma: as a committed Newtonian scientist, he accepted the dogma of the causal determination of the natural world; yet as a moralist, he had to confirm freedom. Resolutely, he pulled together these centrifugal forces in his postulate of God as the Supreme Legislator and Creator of the world, the final sanction of man's conduct. The irony of this position, which his successors tried to escape, was that on the strict terms of his metaphysics of finitude, Kant could not know or prove any of these requirements for the specifically human or moral life. His own premises compelled him to leave man in a state of suspended alienation, with knowledge and speculation divorced from faith and action. Given this situation, we can understand the import of Hegel's remark: "The contrast between faith and reason is in our time a contrast within philosophy itself."[10]

Hegel's resolution of Kant's dichotomy was effected by collapsing the abstractive or categorizing Kantian understanding into the dynamic or dialectical reason. This meant that the Transcendental Logic was absorbed by the Transcendental Dialectic, or more generally that the abstract universals or eternal essences of formal logic became moments or legitimate, yet partial, characterizations of

10. "Glauben und Wissen," in *SW, 1,* 279.

things in the ongoing process of human thought. We must be careful not to do Hegel the injustice of talking as if he denied the validity, or failed to recognize the value, of the abstract and formal procedure of scientific thought. On the contrary, his stress on dialectic—we should note even this word's verbal affinity to dialogue—expressed the insight that for humans, knowing involves an interplay—not an opposition—of abstract and concrete, of universal and particular, of form and content. Kant, to be sure, had discussed knowledge *(Wissen)*; Hegel, by contrast, was interested in philosophical apprehension *(Erkennen)*.

> On the other hand, we speak of "cognition" or philosophical knowledge, when we have knowledge of a Universal, and at the same time comprehend it in its special definite character, and as a connected *whole* in itself.[11]

What Hegel asserted in this rather cryptic sentence was a refusal to dignify with the name of science the wholesale accumulation of facts. Even etymologically science means knowledge traditionally associated with generalization or universalized thought. Hegel shifted the emphasis to the process of universalization since we might construe universal as meaning "one in opposition to others" *(unum versus alia)*. Hegelian science, therefore, is an organizing process; it consists in apprehending items in their interrelatedness. Thus the predominant feature of Hegelian thought is an insistence upon a total point of view; knowledge of a whole system is necessary for a true or adequate understanding of the function of any part.

In order to help us come closer to the totality or unity that is life, Hegel urged that we recognize that even abstraction involves a reciprocity of form ("that which") and ground ("from which"). Therefore he insisted that a concept *(Begriff)* is the activity of comprehending, of holding to-

11. *Lectures on the Philosophy of Religion, 1,* 120–21; *SW, 15,* 132.

gether these two moments, form and ground, in their dynamic relationship.

> To grasp anything in thought means that we conceive of it as a moment of a connected whole, which in its character as a connected whole has the element of difference in it, and has thus a definite and substantial nature.[12]

Significantly, Hegel has used the verbal form, *begreifen*, "to grasp in thought," in order to emphasize an act, as elsewhere he similarly referred to thought activity as *Denken*. In thinking, a man forms a concept. Literally, to "take something with" *(con-cipere)* or fashion a union is the every essence of the thought process. Hence "thought is the activity of the Universal, having a universal as its object."[13] By conceiving something, that is, by taking it as a "moment of a connected whole," we engage in true science: relating, unifying, systematizing, universalizing.

Initially, experience began with our immersion in a world. "Tossed" here, we were constrained to live with and react to "things." It is this moment of immediacy, of unreflected position, which Hegel termed "in itself," for one is completely absorbed in the experience itself. Evidently objects of all kinds are present to us to be treated or handled without their being formally characterized as determinate things-in-themselves. This further determination, the second moment of the dialectic, is in Spinoza's terms that of negation or particularity. The negation consists in knowing the object "for itself"; it has been located or specified in an intelligible world. In the next moment, that of full reflection, we recognize our relationships to objects. We become aware that as subjects we have been thinking about a world: rendering objects intelligible by classifying them as substances of various kinds. Subject and object thus stand

12. Ibid., *2*, 291; *SW*, *16*, 159.
13. Ibid., *1*, 195; *SW*, *15*, 206.

in mutual dependence, in a union of the in-and-for-itself. This comprehensive moment is both a unification of the thought process and a realization. In it the traditional, abstract universal concept and the particular are brought together to constitute the individual or concrete universal, the so-called negation of the negation.

This *individuum,* the concrete or undivided Hegelian universal, fulfilled his specifications for a concept *(Begriff),* since it is a taking or holding together of different or contradictory moments of thought. Thought, then, is concrete or holistic; it "thinks the differences." Technically, it is the process of *Aufhebung,* a word that suggests a suppression or negation of what is partial or fragmentary, a preservation of the negated moment in the conservation of what is essential, and a sublation or sublimation to a higher or more comprehensive level of truth or reality. Because this thought process is to be considered as a dialectical union of form and matter, in contrast to the Kantian formalism in which the power of form (thought) works a unification upon the matter or content of knowledge, Hegel defined philosophical science as the unfolding of this process of making intelligible, or, in technical language, as the exhibition of the concept. In brief, the concept offers us a systematic presentation of reality (the intelligible world).

Hegel's phenomenology, unlike the currently popular Husserlian variety, which owes more to Descartes and Kant in that it aims at unfolding the structures of human consciousness, was a kind of armchair effort at seeing how thought has presented itself in the course of human history. The Egyptian, Oriental, Greek, Roman, and Western European civilizations passed before the philosopher's eye, and of each he asked the critical question: What does knowing or making something intelligible mean? He discovered that it was simply an act of reflection, of realizing progressively what was involved or implied in one's lived experience. There is nothing esoteric in the shibboleth: the real is ra-

tional, the rational is real. In our world only man, traditionally defined as the rational animal, asks questions about
actuality and realization, and he alone seeks to explain
events and to justify his conduct by offering rationalizations
of it. Such rationalizations are of necessity a step behind the
tide of things. In fact, the paradox of thought is that we both
explicate a changing world from an entrenched position and
with an open mind interrogate a logically closed world.

The world does not appear as thought until actuality
has completed its process and constituted itself a finished product. The Notion [*Begriff*] teaches this lesson,
and history can only repeat it; only when actuality is
ripe does the ideal appear over against the real and,
grasping that same real world in its substance, constitutes it in the shape of an intellectual world. When
philosophy paints its gray monochrome, some shape of
life has grown old, and it cannot by this unrelieved
gray be made young again, but only known. The owl
of Minerva takes wing only as the twilight fails.[14]

We shall return to this paradox shortly. For the moment
we must try to catch a glimpse of certain other aspects of
Hegel's vision of reflective thought. He saw dialectic first of
all as a mediation of the Kantian alienation, because the
cleavage of thought and world could be neither a true
starting-point nor end product of the discriminating power
of reasoning. Since thought is a revelatory step back from
an intelligible world, man who is by essence rational actually
finds himself when he uncovers the rational structure of
things. Through understanding, therefore, he is "at home"
in the world—*bei sich.*
Hegel also saw the dialectic as a concrete historical pro-

14, *Grundlinien der Philosophie des Rechts* (4th ed. Hamburg, Felix
Meiner, 1955), Preface, p. 17. The translation is G. R. G. Mure's, in *A Study
of Hegel's Logic* (Oxford, Clarendon Press, 1959), p. 324.

cess. Masters and slaves, for instance, are historical data of social experience. And so twice in his works Hegel elaborated on their dialectical relation in order, first, to clarify their respective positions in terms of the decisive issue of freedom, then to indicate that the personal recognition for which they struggled was itself an evolving phenomenon, and finally, to convince us that, even though we have transcended their limited historical situation, we likewise are engaged in a similar, because essentially human, striving for personal freedom and integrity. Thus the Hegelian process of rendering something intelligible or explaining it is, succinctly stated, an *Erinnerung*. Explication is a movement within or penetration, in this case to the basic core of personality. But by this movement we are caught up in a complicated web or tissue of relations (the etymological sense of history), with the result that our fundamental human situation, our continuity with the past, is called to mind *(erinnern,* "to remember," suggests a movement within). History, then, for Hegel was not the simple fact-gathering of historicism. It was a revelation: the activity of accounting for the past in such a way that it genuinely contributes to the meaningfulness of present experience.

If we are to grasp the import of this last sentence, we must again remind ourselves of the anti-Kantian thrust of Hegelian thought. Educated in physics and optics at a time when these were still attached to the corpus of "natural philosophy," and more than ordinarily partial to Aristotle's biologist mentality, Kant naturally thought of knowledge as a matter of properly categorizing items. No wonder that in spite of all his contortions he could not fit religion, the area of conduct or life, into the intellectual scheme of his First Critique. The Hegelian way out of this impasse was to broaden the rigid idea of knowledge beyond abstract categorizing to dynamic process so that it paralleled the *Rausch* and fluidity of life itself. Rationality, we would say today, had to be thought existentially, not categorically, that is, as the mode of life characteristic of free beings. Moreover, since people must be educated to freedom and trained to think consistently, Hegel rightfully maintained that individually and collectively we pass through stages along the road to maturity. Yet as we know from harsh experience, this maturity is not a once-and-for-all state or condition of complacency. Like life itself it must be lived anew, so that every day we must reconquer the perduring past and draw out new vitality from the abiding possibilities of retrogression within us.

In their genesis, Hegel's ideas about liberty owe much to the French Revolution.[15] But his extensive reading assured him that historiography supported his evaluation, namely, that the growth in a society's rationality spells a commensurate development in its freedom. Surely Hegel has not been the first or only thinker to judge a society's sanity or rational behavior by its response to threats upon its liberty. But more important for our understanding of his treatment of religion is the internal connection he made between freedom and rationality, because Hegel has developed an additional Kantian theme: that freedom of thought is limited by imagination.

An example from contemporary philosophy might clarify this point. Heidegger, with justice perhaps, has been criticized by several classical philologists for excursions into Greek etymology that purportedly deliver to us the Greek "original sense" or "primitive feel" of an utterance. Moreover, he has been criticized, along with Hegel, for indulging a favorite pastime of German philosophers, *Wortspiel*. Less, however, has been said about the significant but unobtrusive suggestions of language that sometimes clarify connections and explain the progression of *Sein und Zeit*. A Kantian impulse, for instance, might account for the phenom-

15. The reader will find some of the pertinent texts on freedom and rationality in my article, "An Interpretation of Hegel's Political Thought," *The Monist, 48* (1964), esp. 101–02.

enological investigation of conscience as a sequel to the examination of the structures of the knowing *Dasein*. But a greater sensitivity to German can reveal to Heidegger's reader allusions or suggestions which he undoubtedly intended. Apparently, *Gewissen* (conscience) quite naturally has been suggested by *Wissen* (knowledge), and mention of the *Ruf* (call) of conscience carries one through a telephone sequence: *anrufen* (to call someone), *holen* (to fetch the party called; Heidegger uses the verb-form, *zurückzuholen*)—which ends at last in the notion of philosophy as a *Wiederholung* (retrieve).

This procedure is open to the objection that phenomenology is an affair of exploring the German consciousness. But by stressing the profoundly Hegelian idea that philosophic knowledge is an inward-moving process of recognition or remembrance, Heidegger has compelled us to come to terms with our universal pretensions and the historically conditioned imaginations which curtail our experience. For this reason he has made much of man's fate *(Schicksal)* and destiny *(Geschick)*. It is because man is thrown or sent *(schicken)* into a particular place of encounter that his human history *(Geschichte)* is a reality. In other words, through philosophical anamnesis one undergoes "psychoanalysis" and is brought face to face with a deeper, more personal and vulnerably human Self. Because this Self is a complexus of social conditioning, the analysis opens our eyes to unexplored realms of psychobiological experience.[16] The act of encounter by which a world is revealed uncovers a nonreflected *prise de position*. Through successive reflections we become aware that because we are already, even at the outset, participants in a world, we exist

16. See Godfrey Lienhardt, *Divinity and Experience: The Religion of the Dinka* (Oxford, at the Clarendon Press, 1961); and Victor W. Turner, "Colour Classification in Ndembu Ritual: A Problem in Primitive Classification," in Michael Banton, ed., *Anthropological Approaches to the Study of Religion* (London, Tavistock Publications, 1966), pp. 47–84.

in anxiety, amid the inevitable tensions of an individual in a group. Man, in this view, becomes man by an act of symbolization. (One can shake out the notion of "encounter" from the Greek συμ-βάλλειν, literally, *to hurl with*.) Concretely he feels, perceives, and lives as he does, as a contemporary German, for instance, because of his mode of experiencing "the world," that is, because of his German imagination. Obviously, we are not using "imagination" to mean the image-making faculty or to talk about the fantastic or unreal. Rather, we understand it somewhat after the fashion in which the medievals talked about the phantasm or Kant spoke of the Transcendental Imagination: as what bridges the concrete and abstract in our thought, as what gives our reasonings their particular tonus, as what sets the horizon for, and therefore limits the scope of, our rational activity.

Hegel's atheistic interpreters have always been ready to exploit the fact that he designated religion's moment of thought as that of *Vorstellung,* a term whose ambiguity is mirrored in its English renditions as "representation," "imagination," even "notion." Since Hegel himself never bothered to be precise (he spoke indiscriminately of *die Vorstellung* and *das Vorstellen* as opposed to thought, of which the verbal form, as in §20 of the *Encyclopedia,* carries the meaning of agent, activity, and product of activity), it is evident that in place of a detailed textual study, the following discussion—limited to the requirements of our theological perspective—pretends to no more than a reasonable interpretation.[17]

In the general context of Hegel's system the doctrine of

17. Unfortunately, the dissertation of Malcolm Clark (Heythrop College, Oxfordshire), "Logic and System: A Study of the Transition from 'Vorstellung' to Thought in the Philosophy of Hegel," University of Louvain, 1960, has not yet been published. An excerpt of this work appeared as "Meaning and Learning in Hegel's Philosophy" in the *Revue philosophique de Louvain,* 58 (1960), 557–78.

Vorstellung is primarily a purely philosophical issue. Immediately, it was the linch-pin of Hegel's reconciliation of the divorce of form from content in Kantian thought, although its historical roots reach back to the Greeks, as Hegel himself acknowledged by citing Aristotle's *Metaphysics* at the end of the *Encyclopedia: ὥστε τἀυτὸν νοῦς καὶ νόητον* ("So that mind and its object are the same"). The disconcerting paradox of thought lies in its nature as a unifying process, for it is a thrust toward "the One" bogged down by an inescapable "Otherness." Only in a mystic One, as Plotinus has shown, do form and content merge completely, but there thought disappears in the night "where all cows are black." Since philosophers traditionally have busied themselves thinking about thought, they have examined the roots of this "otherness" in experience, discussed agent intellects, transcendental structures, and similar devices concocted to explain how thought grows out of experience, and worried over the puzzling dialectical movement from experience to thought, back to experience again. The soft spot in Kant's explication of this process was his difficult (because obscure) notion of schematization of categories, which, as we know particularly from Heidegger's provocative treatment of *Kant and the Problem of Metaphysics,* was accomplished mainly by the Transcendental Imagination.[18] In contemporary language, this is the deli-

18. At the heart of the Kantian philosophy is the problem of restoring universality and necessity to science in the wake of the Humean critique. His thesis, as we know, was that the generality of universal concepts is imposed from the center of apperceptive unity, not extracted from the stuff of sensation. In order, therefore, for the imagination to bridge the gap between the categories and sense phenomena by rendering a category applicable to phenomena, Kant supposed an element homogeneous to both. Analysis disclosed this element, for he uncovered that all the schemata are apriori determinations of time.

Although Kant himself pointed to this chapter on schematism as very important (one of his noted commentators has called it the pivotal piece of the whole *Critique*), it is evident that in his system also the movement from sense to intellect remains mysterious: "a hidden art in the depths of the

cate question of the verification of meaning in existence. We should note that in §454 of the *Encyclopedia* Hegel—in a patently Kantian context since §455 treats of the imagination—has indicated that what he meant by a *Vorstellung* was a synthesis of interior or "mere" signification *(Bild)* with "remembered existence" or designation.[19] Consequently, the doctrine of *Vorstellung* has nothing to do with a contemptibly lower or inferior type of thought. On the contrary, Hegel wished only to emphasize that because philosophy is a thinking about thought (the νόησις νοήσεως), in it alone is form adequate to content.[20] In other disciplines, religion included, the knower takes form for granted because of his absorption in content.

For Hegel the distinctive feature of art and revealed religion, which unlike natural science belong in his system to Absolute Knowledge, was precisely that these disciplines qua self-conscious thought were inextricably linked to philosophy. Philosophy, therefore, cannot be considered an independent subject. As a reflection upon, it is always a movement out of and back into *Vorstellung*, or, perhaps

human soul." The notion of art is suggestive of Hume, who stressed the all important role of *praxis* in the formation of knowledge and habit, and echoes Leibniz, who emphasized that not all is clear calculating within the human spirit since the *petites perceptions* effect a great subterranean work on what appears to be most conscious and clear. Nonetheless, it is unfortunate that at the moment we are most in need of clarity, Kant stated his need to run along, not hesitating over "dry and tedious matter."

19. "This synthesis of inner (mere) signification and remembered existence is, properly speaking, the notion *(Vorstellung)*, in that this inner thing now likewise has the determination of being capable of representation before the intelligence and of having its existence in it."

20. In an interesting explication of the role of *Vorstellung* in which he adverts to Kant's formal *Verstand*, Hegel asseverated: "The difference between *Vorstellung* and Thought has a more precise import, because in general it might be said that the sole purpose of philosophy is to change notions *(Vorstellungen)* into thought; indeed, beyond this, to change pure thoughts into the Concept." *Enzyklopädie der philosophischen Wissenschaften* (1830 edit.), §20.

more accurately, it is the movement of which the process
of *vorstellen* (literally, to place before) forms an integral
part. Through this process of rational thought we come to a
genuine self-consciousness: to the awareness or realization
that religion, for all of its talk about God and similar facts,
reveals to us the meaning of ourselves and our world. If this
is the case, the purpose of emphasizing religion as the moment of *Vorstellung* is to show clearly that it is in origin and
development an experience, for hallucinations and self-
engendered imaginings are not authentic presentations.
And because revealed religion is irrevocably bound to its
inaugural epiphanies, to the hierophanies which authenticate its inspiration, it is unavoidably expressed in the mythic
and symbolic languages which testify to these experiential
groundings.

Interestingly, the sinuousness of Hegel's discussion,
owing to its imbrication with Kantian themes, can illuminate the problem of the contemporary philosopher who
attempts to enter into the current debate over myths and
symbols. For before the philosopher can bring his epistemological and hermeneutical interests to bear on this conflict, he must come to grips with the arduous and exceeding-
ly controversial task of definition. Just as Hegel defined key
terms with reference to his peculiar system and built into
them an anti- or preter-Kantian stance, so does every dis-
putant over myth and symbol. In most cases religious symbols function against the background of a complex system
of beliefs about supernatural beings, a system which, need-
less to say, furnishes the material for the requisite identifi-
cations of objects symbolized. Thus no one can talk
significantly about these symbols and myths unless he is
prepared to fit them into their proper *Lebenswelt*—that
complex of experience which permits one to speak meaningfully about both facets of the dialectic, "natural and
supernatural," "symbolic and nonsymbolic," "mythical and
nonmythical." In other words it will not do either heuris-

tically or epistemologically, to label man the "symbolic animal" as if we were relieved thereby from the onerous duty of specifying the referents of our symbols. Only in Cloudland is everything symbolic.

A symbol, as we shall understand it in this work, belongs to the genus of sign; it points toward or refers to. But as distinguished from a mere sign which exhausts its function in bare pointing, that is, in simple direction-indicating— "Slow," "Los Angeles–235 miles," "Tailor"—the symbol directs our manner of thinking about an object. By stating, for example, that a shepherd is an apt symbol for God, we have meant traditionally that the idea of shepherd conditions our approach to God; it gears the mind to think of His providence and divine care. No doubt this dimension of symbolism clarifies what Kant understood by the imaginative schematization of a category, or what Gendlin has designated as "felt meaning."

Yet it is not sufficient to characterize a symbol by its feeling component. Since even our "objective" thought, which pretends to a straightforward categorizing of things as they are, is recognized today as a process of "seeing as," it is, as a consequence, intermingled with ever-present, though perhaps not openly avowed, attitudes or anticipations. Until recently it has been stylish in many quarters to dismiss images, symbols, and myths as playthings of poets, religious believers, and primitives, on the score that the fanciful has no rational relevance to man's spiritual–intellectual life. Intoxicated with Reason, the extollers of man's rationality apparently never learned enough Hegel to come to suspect that they might be foisting upon us a novel, yet unadulterated, myth—or at best a heady but diluted abstraction. For does not the reciprocal dialectical movement between *Vorstellung* and thought, between symbolization and rationality, embody the very paradox of thought itself? Rational cognition, by dint of its function as critic of presentative thought seeks, so to say, to alienate itself from, and would deny if it could, its own origins. Yet by taking a step out of the imaginative in order to judge it, rational knowledge forges an indestructible link with its counterpart. In no other way can life become verified experience. It is precisely this subtle circular or dialectical movement that the word σύμβολον was originally meant to designate. Primarily, the word meant a sign of recognition: the part of a divided object that an individual retained in order to be recognized by another. Thus the word symbol has built into it, and that not merely from its verbal etymology, συμ-βάλλειν, the notion of an encounter: a meeting in which divergent elements or parts come together or unify, literally make an acknowledged unity in which diversity or otherness is an essential moment. Concretely, then, unlike the sign, which designates as unequivocally as possible, the symbol points in the peculiar negative way of thought itself. It tells us how to take the object to which we are "related" (God as shepherd in our example), but emphasizes both the fittingness and inadequacy of this mode of relationship. God is only like a shepherd, and that is not the unique way of thinking about Him.

It is almost a truism that our perplexities over symbols stem from our uncertainties about ourselves as men. In the Western, Greek-inspired philosophical tradition, man has been defined as a rational being, which generally has been understood in a rationalistic Aristotelian or Kantian sense. The human intellect was "divine," for its crowning achievement was a grasp of eternal essences and a rigorous, neatly compartmentalized science. Notwithstanding all the lip service paid to the idea that it is man who knows, the tendency among Western thinkers has been to belittle all who do not know in their peculiarly abstract fashion. Naturally, symbolic thought, which as Hegel intimated is a harmonizing or reconciling activity because it is the function of a reasoning power conceived in terms of the whole man, had to be trivialized and eventually denigrated to the unsophisticated level of a debased imagination. Instead of retaining its status, therefore, as the uniquely proper mode of human expression, symbolic thought became only a mode of conception or speech of which man is capable—and that quite unreliable. In brief it was easier to identify it with pictorial thought than to grapple with its problems, which are deeply rooted in human nature. If man himself is a rational animal, composed of "heaven and earth," the place of encounter of Absolute and contingent, an image or shadow of God, all of his basic activities are marked by his radical ambivalence. It is the symbol, born in and for an encounter, that mirrors the dialectic of the dependence–independence, the temporality–eternality of his nature. Symbolism, then, cannot be escaped: it is the phenomenal manifestation of the fundamental human image.

If we allow ourselves in this manner to think the symbol ontologically, and man himself as the primordial symbol, then we are in a position to understand some of the more abstruse facets of the Kantian–Hegelian–Heideggerian thought: specifically the intimate connection between negativity, imagination, time, and finitude. Only then will we be ready to approach the complicated topic of myth. Kant, as we know, was interested in discovering and explicating the transcendental structures that make experience possible. Central to man's phenomenal (abstractive, and therefore negating) thought was the operation of the Transcendental Imagination in conjunction with the form of the inner sense, time. His language may suggest to us an artificial "metaphysics of finitude"; but looked at from another viewpoint it is a careful and thoughtful attempt to analyze and synthesize the peculiarities of our ordinary experience. As Wittgenstein might have warned us, nobody has problems with "experience" until he begins to ask questions about it. For every experience is something individual, personal, marked by what Heidegger would call *Jemeinigkeit*. And yet in order for it to be identifiable and intelligible qua personal experience, a person must learn to classify it. The individual, therefore, is persistently universal or other-related. Moreover, whatever one experiences, he designates as part of his experience; it must fit in or relate to the totality of his lived experience. Finally, experience is over-whelmingly immediate in its actuality, and yet we do not know it or realize it until it is already past. The upshot of these reflections—that experience is a dialectical transcen-dence of whole and part, of now and then—is that the negativity which constitutes the act of transcendence or thought is intrinsically dependent upon the structure of temporality, that is, what allows the possibility of phenom-enal time (appropriately called by Sartre the "power of Negation") and accomplished through the activity of the imagination.[21] In German, the word for imagination, *Einbildungskraft,* is more suggestive of this activity, since it might be translated with equal right as "the informing power" or the "acculturating force."

If we have clearly understood what it means to be "formed into" something by this "visible making" activity (the Greek sense of φαντάζειν), or to be inserted into a culture, then we are better able to appreciate how this negating power is the root of our sense of time precisely because it enables us to leap beyond immediacy in order to apprehend temporal sequence. Only symbolic man can transcend the immediate by negating it, and so it is only man qua symbol who is caught in time's web of history. Natural-ly, therefore, he forges a dynamic system of symbols, arche-types, and schemes that witness to his acculturation. These

21. In order to understand Heidegger's discussion in *Sein und Zeit,* pp. 424 ff. (English translation, pp. 477 ff.), one should look briefly at Hegel's *Die Vernunft in der Geschichte,* the Meiner Philosophische Bibliothek edi-tion, pp. 153 and 178, and then see how he has developed these thoughts more systematically in §258 of the *Encyclopedia.* Ultimately, one is back to the problem of the *Wissenschaft der Logik* (Meiner Verlag, Lasson edit.), 2, 15–16: the position as presupposition. For Sartre, these discussions are basic to *L'être et le néant,* pp. 30–34, and p. 716.

are the myths that help him to render an account of himself and his world and, within a religious purview, are reenacted in time-transcending ritual and cultic celebrations. This ontological or anthropological consideration of symbols would seem to be confirmed by the more phenomenological analyses of the professional ethnologists and historians of religions. For example the wealth of images studied by Mircea Eliade in his *Patterns in Comparative Religion* brings him to the conclusion that

> symbolism appears to be a "language" understood by all the members of the community and meaningless to outsiders, but certainly a "language" expressing at once and equally clearly the social, "historic" and psychic condition of the symbol's wearer, and his relations with society and the cosmos.[22]

Here we find the principal features of our analysis: the phenomenon of acculturation; and the negative, or dialectical, element present in the individual's act of self-transcendence both of the immediate group and toward wider participation in that group's history. The temporal nature of this transcendence figures more prominently in Eliade's description of a religious symbol as deriving its force from an original hierophany. It is a prolongation of an hierophany because it mediates an experience to those who were not present at the initial manifestation. Because of this revelatory function, the symbol is especially suited to articulate myths.

If modesty is the virtue becoming the investigator of symbols, then nothing less than extreme caution should grace the researcher of myths. When dealing with such a complex cultural phenomenon it is practically impossible to find a definition or description capable of satisfying all the experts. Ethnologists, anthropologists, historians of religions, theologians, philosophers, and literary critics have

22. Meridian Books edition (Cleveland, World Publishing, 1963), p. 451.

been guided by their respective interests and tend to formulate definitions which, although often complementary, emanate from and enhance their limited horizons.[23] For our purposes, the important element in the description of myth is, as Alan Watts has pointed out,[24] that a complex of stories or a narrative demonstrates for man the inner meaning of the universe and human life. Hence Eliade has emphasized that myth narrates a "sacred history":

> not only the origin of the world, of animals, of plants, and of man, but also all the primordial events in consequence of which man became what he is today— mortal, sexed, organized in a society, obliged to work in order to live, and working in accordance with certain rules.[25]

In a word, a myth as a symbolic scheme is also to be understood as essentially a revelatory structure. Since it, too, enables man to grasp his situation in its totality, it should be viewed as both the natural expression and fulfillment of his symbolic nature.

We have described the dynamism of the symbol as a dialectic: a holding together of the immediate with its correlative nonimmediate horizon, a grasp of the part in its necessary relationship to the whole. Understanding, as Kant recognized, cannot operate without a limiting, ideal-setting Reason. And because thought and language, as both Wittgenstein and Heidegger have pointed out, are insep-

23. David Bidney, "Myth, Symbolism, and Truth," in *Myth: A Symposium,* Thomas A. Sebeok, ed. (Bloomington, Indiana University Press, Midland Book edition, 1965), pp. 3–24, has a short, informative rundown of theories about myth, although the author himself subscribes to the view that myth originates "wherever thought and imagination are employed uncritically or deliberately used to promote social delusion."

24. In *Myth and Ritual in Christianity* (New York, Vanguard, 1954), p. 7, cited by Philip Wheelwright in *Myth: A Symposium,* p. 154.

25. *Myth and Reality,* Eng. trans. Willard R. Trask (New York, Harper & Row, 1963), pp. 11, 5.

arable in that expression is the only adequate criterion of thought, the myth is an inevitable constituent of human existence. This conclusion, to be sure, will be shocking only to those who are convinced that we outgrew mythopoeic thought with the loincloth. But they need to be reminded— Eliade has proved to be the psychopomp *par excellence* of this region—of the survival of myths in camouflage and of the degenerated rituals which are commonplace in our civilization: housewarmings, marriage and birth rites, New Year's festivities, television fare of fights between "good" and "bad" or heroes and monsters, dreams of paradisial settings, of Marxist utopias, of escapes into the underworld, even efforts to "kill time" by absorption in novels, detective stories, and movies.[26] No wonder Jung postulated unconscious "objectives" or archetypes to explain these universally recurring themes of man's history. At least he tried to take seriously the fact that mankind has always been tortured by the longing to break through the temporal and ontological constrictions of the human condition.

For us who are inhabitants of a psychology oriented world, there is something disturbing about the suggestion of an escape from the "real" through the abolition of time. We tend to confuse this with a pathological flight from one's problems or with the fantasy world of *As You Like It* or another piece of pastoral literature. Similarly, a religious representation of creative acts or of deeds perpetrated by a mythical hero or ancestor *in illo tempore* is apt to strike us as a "primitive" attempt to turn back the clock. How can participation in these ritual repetitions effect the regeneration of "the world" and a people? We cannot suppose that Hegel had the resources at hand to enable him to forge the link between his intellectualized treatment of *Vorstellung*

26. Eliade returns to this theme frequently in his works. See, for instance, the papers collected in *Myth and Reality* and *Myths, Dreams and Mysteries: The Encounter between Contemporary Faiths and Archaic Realities*, Eng. trans. Philip Mairet (New York, Harper & Row, 1960).

and the fruitful notion of myth as exemplary history. But
has he not shown us not only that there is nothing unreal
about the activity of *vorstellen* but that it is an essential,
though paradoxical, component of man's rational activity?
Moreover, his purpose in displaying the trajectory of the
human spirit was to present us with an authentic phenomenology, that is, a striking manifestation or compelling exposition of how we appear now because, in some strange way,
ontogenesis has recapitulated phylogenesis. We sum up in
ourselves the whole history of our race. Consequently, whoever would understand himself must necessarily remember.
He must perform an authentic act of going in *(Erinnerung)*,
not just of recalling a number of past facts, so that what he
really is might be revealed. "Philosophical *anamnesis*,"
Eliade has noted in a discussion of Plato,

> does not recover the memory of the *events* belonging to
> former lives, but of *truths*, that is, of the structures of
> the real. This philosophical position can be compared
> with that of the traditional societies: the myths repre-
> sent paradigmatic models established by supernatural
> beings not the series of personal experiences of one
> individual or another.[27]

Although Hegel, as a philosopher, has pointed in general
to the basic paradox of symbolic man's thinking activity, he
has not discussed the problem of myth understood in a
more technical sense, particularly insofar as it concerns the
philosopher of religion or theologian. For both Lévi-Strauss'
structural approach to myth interpretation and the plethora
of material assembled by Eliade for his morphological and
phenomenological construction would seem to confirm the
thesis which Gilbert Durand has argued with a super-
abundance of examples: that the great symbolic regimes of

---

27. "Mythologies of Memory and Forgetting." *History of Religions*, 2
(1963), 336.

the imagination, the diurnal and nocturnal, the heroic and the mysterious, the ascending and the descending, exist to provide man with a reason to live and a reason to die.[28] According to this analysis, the primordial function of man's "fantastic power" is one of euphemizing his destiny. Myth, then, is to be considered as an exposé of the method by which mankind, to the degree that it can, reestablishes an order for limiting the effects of death. Within this purview, all of our scientific or metaphysical thought, indeed all objective thought, is derivative, abstract, impoverished.

Such a description of mythic thought has much to recommend it since it can rely on the data of Jung and Piaget in support of the continuity, that is to say, the solidarity or functional coherence of man's form of representation, specifically his symbolic thought and conceptual meaning. It emphasizes the essential creativity of man's intellectual enterprise, for "insight" and "genius" are rightfully attributed to minds that are singularly "imaginative." Gusdorf, for instance, has shown the ontological consequences of the geometrical (circular) consideration of time (the relationship of *annus* to *annulus*), and has offered serious reasons for considering astrobiology as the basis for the human idea of the cosmos, either in the form of the Hindu *Rta*, the Chinese *Tao*, the Greek *Moira*, or of the modern idea of an intelligible whole. The important point is that these models, insofar as they determine an entire heuristic attitude, are the dynamically creative images of human understanding.

It should be evident that in describing myth or *Vorstellung* in this functional way we have in mind a spiraling assimilation–accommodation scheme of the kind Piaget has suggested because it accounts for the impact of the "contradictions" of lived experience upon the correction and/or

28. *Les structures anthropologiques de l'imaginaire: Introduction à l'archétypologie générale* (2nd ed. Paris, Presses universitaires de France, 1963).

development of our cognitive structures. Yet it is at this juncture that the fundamental paradox of mythic thought causes embarrassment. For within this complex of human creativity and understanding is born the critical faculty which, to the degree that it becomes rationalistic or "scientific," turns upon its origins and labels them "fantastic" in the pejorative sense. What is the validity of these imaginative models which are the heuristic inspirations of our world? Does the intelligible world provide direct evidence for its inaugurating conceptions? Thought, as Hegel has shown us, breeds its contradictories. Therefore myths, precisely because they are revelatory of a world's meaning, are subject to all of man's fretting over reasonable certitude and security. And so we are brought to the inevitable paradox: notwithstanding the obvious continuity of mythic and conceptual thought, we are forced to stress their discontinuity. As Jensen has noted,

> Genuine mythic cognition makes statements about the nature of reality for which there cannot be any comparable scientific statements; the methods of science are oriented toward a different nature of reality, toward the quantitative and measurable which is never understood through direct impression but only by the detour of de-anthropomorphization."[29]

Because religion offers man a holistic view of things—it anthropomorphizes him by situating him in a meaningful world and involving him in ritual acts which commemorate or celebrate his destiny—it clearly belongs to the category of mythic cognition. Today, certainly, most theologians would accept this classification provided that the term "myth" is cleared of the misunderstandings and polemics of Modernism and that one is not committed thereby to a pro-

29. Adolf E. Jensen, *Myth and Cult Among Primitive Peoples*, Eng. trans. Marianna Tax Choldin and Wolfgang Weissleder (Chicago, University of Chicago Press, 1963), p. 324.

gram of Bultmannian demythologizing. Actually, both of
these provisos are bound up with Jensen's word, reality,
since the tendency of demythologizers, from the early
Greek philosophers through the *philosophes* and *Aufklärer*
to our contemporary advocates of modern science, has been
to relegate everything that does not conform to their
restricted norms of rationality to the wastebasket of delusion. In practice, all of our knowledge, including that of
natural science which, qua science, is distinguished by a
degree of universality, involves the act of negating transcendence that is characteristic of mythic thought. Consequently, the controversy over religious myth is not one over
man's attempted abolition of time and escape from the
immediate but of the nature of the "world" to which one
transcends. Hence the task of the theologian, if he is to hold
his ground against all forms of reductionism, is to describe a
significant world that remains impervious to these attempts
at naturalistic transposition. In brief, he cannot, as Eliade
has pointed out, lose the actions of Supernatural Beings in
the revelatory function of myths.

Perhaps this point can be illustrated by noting the contrast between the Christian theologian's idea of religion as
a self-revelation of God which clarifies man's self-under-
standing and the social anthropologist's notion which may,
for the purposes of definition, refer to an "institution consisting of culturally patterned interaction with culturally
postulated superhuman beings," but which, methodologi-
cally, is limited to the investigable aspects of human self-
comprehension.[30] On principle, the theologian cannot be
opposed to any investigation of his area which promises significant information. Since it is generally acknowledged that
every comprehensive human value system is studded with all
the complexities of life itself, do we not stand to profit from

30. Melford E. Spiro, "Religion: Problems of Definition and Explanation," in Banton, ed., *Anthropological Approaches*, p. 96.

the piecemeal approach to religion? Surely there are definite advantages to studying it as a socially integrating force, as a motivational complex, as an intellectually satisfying answer to the problems of pain and injustice, or even as a normalized outlet for pent-up emotions. But what is uppermost in the mind of the theologian is that this apparent pluralism should not be just a façade. After all, he has learned from Henri Frankfort that the multiplicity of approaches characterizing mythic thought safeguards the integrity of mutually conflicting viewpoints.[31] Yet when he reads Geertz's definition of religion—"a system of symbols which acts to establish powerful, pervasive and long-lasting moods and motivations in men by formulating conceptions of a general order of existence and clothing these conceptions with such an aura of factuality that the moods and motivations seem uniquely realistic"[32]—he wonders whether this perspective from which every reference to any kind of god has been eliminated is not in reality a return to the Greek unitary concept of knowledge and experience. Religion, like science, is a human response, and is, therefore, replete with man's creativity. But to suggest by definition that it is only a human projection, and not a response to a bona fide transcendent experience, is to deny the theologian's major premise. Not even the philosopher would be guilty of this insult. Presumably, he has learned the lesson of Plato's *Theaetetus* (146A–147A): that one cannot establish scientifically that there is truth. One can only begin with the supposition, if

31. See his *Ancient Egyptian Religion: An Interpretation* (New York, Columbia University Press, 1948), and his *Kingship and the Gods: A Study of Ancient Near Eastern Religion as the Integration of Society and Nature* (Chicago, University of Chicago Press, 1948).
32. Clifford Geertz, "Religion as a Cultural System," in Banton, ed., *Anthropological Approaches*. Also found in the *Reader in Comparative Religion: An Anthropological Approach*, William A. Leese and Evon Z. Vogt, eds. (2nd ed. New York, Harper & Row, 1965).

knowledge then truth, and so proceed to a description of the conditions of knowledge. As a critical, reflective activity, philosophy's role is to proffer dialectical solutions of life's paradoxes. But in the name of what ought to be, it cannot and does not disintegrate the very stuff of paradox, such as the word of faith spoken in responsibility.

Historically, of course, the pretensions of philosophers have not been so modest, and theologians have been justifiably suspicious of attempts at "understanding" that are scarcely distinguishable from reductionist efforts to explicate what religious doctrines or concepts "really mean." Admittedly, the line to be drawn is a fine one, so that it should not strike us as unusual that the imputation of heresy was made in regard to Aquinas as it was in respect to Hegel. Anyone, in fact, who chooses the road (Aquinas' traditional arguments are *viae*) of intellectual proofs for God can be assured of a careful scrutiny. "Are you justified in asserting that your Uncaused Cause or Prime Mover is actually 'what we mean by God'?" "On what grounds do you associate the ultimate horizon required in a dialectic of knowledge with the absolute 'Other' needed for the dialectic of faith?" "How does the Christian avoid a pantheistic thralldom?" "Do not the philosophical revolts of Hume, Kierkegaard, Sartre, and Camus point to the real danger of being drowned in a tidal wave of logical totality?" These problems, one would suppose, are endemic to our Western tradition, which can free itself from its Greek leading strings only with the greatest difficulty. And yet, for all of his indebtedness to the Greeks, Hegel was the philosopher who, for our times, has liberated us from their monolithic rationalism. For this reason, if for no other, his thought warrants consideration by religious thinkers.

Hegel began within the congenial premises of Greek thought: the supposition of the organic unity of the cosmos with its intellectual or epistemological counterpart of a mind becoming all things. Plotinus solidified this tradition for later Greek philosophy, and passages of his *Enneads* may strike the present-day reader as peculiarly Hegelian.[33] Yet because this thrust toward a total grasp was the frustrated goal of Kant's philosophy, Hegel, as we know, surveyed the field of thought for hints on how to repair the old scheme of totality or on how to erect a new one. Neither Spinoza's pantheistic world, which only stirred up haunting phantoms of evil and freedom, nor the Lockean-Berkeleian world of logical implication was adequate for reconciling the data at hand. In fact, the very paradox that Hegel uncovered was that the totality presupposed by thought was not "out there" in Spinoza's world or "in here" in the logical world. Like the cheshire cat, it was nowhere yet everywhere; presupposed as motive and goal of man's thoughtful leap, but never comprehended so that the venture of thought was at an end. For us who have lived through Sartre's *The Words*, Hegel's insight that this "cunning of reason" is a play for freedom rings true. We know from experience the agony of breaking out of a world *tout fait*. Inserted into a language community which, for the sake of communication, controls the availability of our concepts and instills in us a code of acceptable behavior, we are compelled to find our authentic selves. We must create ourselves as genuine individuals who are responsible for their thoughts and take the consequences of their values. Yet we cannot do this by rebellion, for we cut ourselves off from the channels of personal development and plunge headlong into chaotic rootlessness.

How, then, does one rationalize this enigmatic freedom?

33. "Lassen had already pointed out that, in Plotinus, the procedures preparatory to ecstasy were remarkably similar to those of Buddhism and the various Brahmanic systems." Cited, together with other pertinent references, by Mircea Eliade from Marcel Mauss, "Rapports historiques entre la mystique hindoue et la mystique occidentale," in *Yoga: Immortality and Freedom,* Eng. trans. Willard R. Trask, Bollingen Series 56 (2nd ed. New York, Pantheon Books, 1958), p. 432.

Hegel, obviously, was convinced that we cannot. Yet he believed that it was more honest to face unflinchingly a surd or mystic One at the beginning of philosophizing than to postpone indefinitely the final accounting. It is easy for us to become preoccupied with the pressing problems of the moment and work ourselves into the frame of mind that all we need to find is a piecemeal approach and convenient ad hoc solutions. Certainly there is nothing wrong about patchwork; it serves a notable pragmatic purpose. But we ought not lose the vision of the whole cloth—at least Hegel has tried to prevent this disaster. For the merit of his entire phenomenology of the human spirit is that it shows us clearly the consequences when one carries our Western option for the Greek mind to its logical extreme. The lesson is patent: thought is a wonderful tool but a tyrannous master.

Our exposure to other cultures has reenforced Hegel's message. We have come to recognize that as Westerners our entire act of existence, as Heidegger has emphasized, is an anomalous choice. The circumstances of education and communication have imposed a viewpoint upon us; the projected totality of our thought is in large measure circumscribed by our particular language and whole cultural situation. But there are meaningful alternatives, and the freedom of our commitment is evinced in our obligation to broaden through criticism the scope of our forced options. This is the decisive issue for the contemporary philosopher of religion. Formerly, the philosophical theologian had to deal with a peculiar form of "Forgetfulness of Being" in that he was pushed to reconcile a religious ideal of what ought to be with the cold reality of what really is. Today, however, Western theology must meet a more basic challenge. For if the structures of the imagination that shape our cognitive models and inject us with a daily modicum of optimism— Tomorrow will always be better—are essentially intercultural phenomena, then we face the far more exacting task of rationalizing the uniqueness of our religious claims. How, in other words, can a personal commitment to a system of truth stand muster with a realistic ecumenism? In the chapters that follow we shall be attempting to come to grips with this problem.

SIX. THE ANALYSIS OF RELIGIOUS DISCOURSE

The confusions which occupy us arise when
language is like an engine idling, not when it
is doing work.

WITTGENSTEIN, *Philosophical Investigations,*
§*132*

If, as Hegel argued, reflective thought uncovers at the
core of our rationality a surd we would not have suspected
in the course of day-to-day living, then undoubtedly this
incomprehensibility will be mirrored in thought's expression. Were not Wittgenstein's *Investigations* conducted
with this in mind, namely, to show us that communication
works well until we become curious about its groundings?
Because foundations are supposed, explanations tend at
some point to become unhinged. For this reason a group
of English philosophers became disillusioned some time ago
by the flimsiness of one *word* standing behind another (as a
piece of outmoded Russellian metaphysics would have them
think) and were saved from complete skepticism only by
their sound, pragmatic common sense. Nonetheless, the
yearning for ultimates or origins is still a characteristic of
an impressively large group of accredited thinkers. Phenomenologists, for example, pursue the original and originating experience which lays claim to be an authentic
Urphänomen. In this they are not above the common cut
of theoreticians who would, if it were possible, formulate
the world in a trice.

In traditional Western thought the discipline to which
one submitted in order to free himself from loose expres-

sion was called *Dialectica,* a name which indicates that what
we know as logic was deeply rooted in, if not engendered by,
the eristic practice of rhetoric. The term dialectic had a
checkered history even within the Peripatetic tradition
in which it figured prominently and from which our notion
of logic as the power ($\delta\dot{\nu}\nu\alpha\mu\iota s$) or art ($\tau\dot{\epsilon}\chi\nu\eta$) of making valid
inferences has been derived. For our purpose, the signifi-
cance of this tradition has been its attention to knowing
as a form of speaking—an ambiguity written into the word
logos itself—and its gradual evolution from a purely formal
to a full-blown epistemological enterprise.[1]

Metaphysicians from Aristotle through the Scholastics,
Leibniz, Wolff, and up to the present have normally commenced speculation by attempting to fix concepts in definitions. Further reflection carried them deeper within
themselves as they grasped the implications of the cognitive
situation. But the controlling moment has been, literally,
the essential one: that determination of the limits of a concept which made further knowledge possible. Thereafter
the metaphysicians could worry about criteria of correct-
ness, specifically about those rules governing the coherence
of expressions, which keep syllogisms free from error. To
achieve this exactness they learned formal logic, whose dry-
ness they have tolerated only because of logic's declared
propaedeutic value.

With Kant's attempted reconstruction of metaphysics a
discordant note was introduced into this harmonious dis-
tribution of roles. He named his new science of the *logos* a
Transcendental Logic because it transcended formal rules
and considered the concept as knowledge of a content.
"That logic," he wrote in the preface to the second edition
of his *Critique of Pure Reason,*

1. For a more thorough treatment, see William and Martha Kneale, *The
Development of Logic,* and Hermann Glockner, *Der Begriff in Hegels Philosophie. Versuch einer logischen Einleitung in das metalogische Grund-
problem des Hegelianismus* (Tübingen, Mohr, 1924).

should have been thus successful is an advantage which it owes entirely to its limitations, whereby it is justified in abstracting—indeed, it is under the obligation to do so—from all objects of knowledge and their differences, leaving the understanding nothing to deal with save itself and its form. But for reason to enter on the sure path of science is, of course, much more difficult, since it has to deal not with itself alone but also with objects.[2]

Having nodded in the direction of what we would call today semantics, Kant spelled out clearly his intention of strolling down this path of science, which consisted in disclosing the ego's cognitive structures.

Such a science, which should determine the origin, the scope, and the objective validity of such knowledge, would have to be called *transcendental logic,* because, unlike general logic, which has to deal with both empirical and pure knowledge of reason, it concerns itself with the laws of understanding and of reason solely in so far as they relate *apriori* to objects.[3]

The temper of the times at the end of the eighteenth century and the beginning of the nineteenth was favorable to this Kantian science so that the transition to Hegelian logic or metaphysics was accomplished without incident. Fichte washed the formalism out of conceptualization by referring to the *Begriff* as the activity of comprehension *(Umgreifen).* And the prevailing mood of romanticism, of which Schelling's *Bruno* is a classic example, helped to popularize Schlegel's disparagement of formal logic and empirical psychology as philosophical monstrosities.

Among continental European metaphysicians who philosophize in the tradition of Kant and Hegel, this evolu-

2. Kant, *Critique of Pure Reason,* Eng. trans. Norman Kemp Smith (London, Macmillan, 1958), p. 18.

3. Ibid., pp. 96–97.

tion from formal to material logic or epistemology has not
been reversed. Both Merleau-Ponty and Heidegger, for instance, each in his own way to be sure, have offered us an
ontological interpretation of *das Wort, Sprache, Rede, langage* and *parole,* a phenomenology, in other words, of logos
aimed at displaying it as a revelatory structure. The activity
of logos indicates to us not only what man is (the traditional
notion of rational animal or incarnate spirit is reflected in
the fact that a physical word conveys a "spiritual" meaning)
but also how man "becomes." He is born into a community
because he is made for communication, for communion
even—provided he is to achieve himself as a well-integrated
person. Heidegger, we have noted, has tried to explore consciousness and thought patterns by attending to the nuances
of German expression, principally by citing etymologies or
constructing (rather dubious) word associations. However
we may judge his effort, it has the merit of highlighting the
reciprocal functions of the two aspects of logos, rationality
and communication, and brings home to us the now commonplace truth that a language is a way of life. Since no one
becomes fully man except through participation in a community, how is he to avoid celebrating his community
through all of his activities: his gestures, his language, and,
in some societies, his ritual actions performed in the service
of the god of the community?

    This type of analysis can reward the Christian theologian
with a number of valuable insights. Educated by the Old
Testament to the concept of the "people of God" and by the
New Testament to the notion of the Church as a community
of faithful, the theologian readily comes to look on faith
as the Word of God spoken and responded to by man as
analogous to an ordinary word of human speech. It is that
which inserts a person into a group of believers, schools him
in its *lingua franca,* and patterns him to think with the
Church and to share its mysteries and communings. Suggestive as this approach may be, however, it does not help

the theologian resolve the problem of seeing beyond his group. He is still confronted with the anomaly of his universal claims couched in a particular language. Inevitably he speaks from within a context to a context.

Before turning to the other genre of contextual analysis, we should remark the peculiarity of having partisans of two styles of thought laying claim to "doing" the logic of religion. The philosopher of a scientific turn of mind looks for the benefits of formalization: precision of thought and rigor of demonstration. The phenomenologist, on the other hand, studies language for deeper insights into the structures of consciousness. In practice, his ultimate criterion of evidence can only be formulated in a personally appealing way: "Does this manner of looking at, and talking about, things make the situation more intelligible to you?" Unfortunately, it is not wholly satisfactory to account for these opposing allegiances by appealing to different tastes or inclinations of mind. Yet what else will do as the final word?

As a prelude to the "scientific" forms of contemporary analysis, the theologian might profitably familiarize himself with some of the more recent developments in linguistics, not merely because there are philosophers who would like to harass him with the suggestion that the findings in this field are disastrous for a theology of universal pretensions, but also because, pragmatically, we are living more and more in "one world," and the minister of the Word can garner from this science much worthwhile information for his mission: suggestions, for example, about terminology, definition, vernacular, and means of communication. Few of us are actually called upon to experience the difficulties of the missionary in Northern Chad who wished to translate Christian concepts into Sara. But we must be prepared to cope with his problem in a serious intellectual fashion, for the missionary sought theological reassurance that his formulations were authentic "translations" of credal statements and longed for the practical certitude that his converts "understood" his message in the way that he understood it.[4]

Briefly, since de Saussure, most linguists have described language *(langage)* as that faculty of human speech which involves psychological and physiological factors in the individual and results in physical, acoustic (or, once removed, graphic) activity. Of more theological pertinence is *langue*, which we might usefully define as a complete, systematically working set of linguistic conventions which characterize any given language. It embraces both the full scope of a community's usage and "the system" which we teach to prospective learners of the tongue. The complex of habits that comprises a langue is what the technical linguist breaks down into a grammatical system (a stock of morphemes and their arrangements), a phonological system (a stock of phonemes and their arrangements), a morphophonemic system (the set of rules for the conjunction of the two previous systems), and two peripheral subsystems, namely, the semantic system (generally, the relationship of words to things; more specifically, the association of morphemes and their combinations with things and situations) and the phonetic system (the ways in which sequences of phonemes are converted into sound waves by the articulation of the speaker—his utterance or *parole*—and decoded from this signal by the hearer).

The area of linguistics most likely to intrigue the philosopher of religion and theologian is semantics, with a notable difference of perspective, however, from that of the scientific linguist or semanticist. As such, the semanticist is interested in how language parcels out reality, and therefore his science or theory is concerned with 'meaning' in several senses. He distinguishes, for instance, linguistic meaning (where the frame of reference is exclusively the language system itself) from equivalence meaning (the determination

4. Jacques Hallaire, "Ils parleront de nouvelles langues," *Christus, 12* (1965), 251–88.

of whether two utterances mean "the same"), and referential meaning to the extent that referents are reflected in language (the study, as Colin Cherry has defined it, "of the non-causal, imputed relations [rules] between *signs* and designata").[5] Theologian and philosopher are likewise involved in referential meaning, but in the interests of experiential verification and adequacy, as well as for the obvious reason that some kind of value judgment is operative when one determines what the linguistic component of a referent is or what might constitute linguistically significant behavior. Essentially, the concentrated focus of the philosopher and theologian is on the extra-linguistic or experiential factors which are always part of the complex of meaningful discourse.

It is the philosopher in the semanticist that may prompt him to suggest a theory of meaning, as opposed to the logician whose classifications are consistently of the black and white variety: objective and subjective, communicative and incommunicative, complete and incomplete, etc.[6] At present, the theory in vogue is contextualization since it avoids the difficulties of the extreme views, both the purely mental and the purely observational types of meaning explanation. Dictionaries, for instance, provide us with an immediate verbal context 'for locating a word's meaning. But at any given moment of use a number of factors converge to form that immediate situational context which highlights the level of utterance—grammatical, phonological, or lexical—on which a meaning functions. Observable antecedents and consequents of the speech act are as relevant to a meaning context as individual psychological factors, and beyond these stands a whole culture: a history that unobtrusively comes to light in delicate shadings and

5. *On Human Communication: A Review, A Survey, and a Criticism* (New York, Science Editions, Inc., 1961), p. 306.
6. See, for example, Joseph Bochenski's *The Logic of Religion* (New York, New York University Press, 1965), pp. 26 ff.

fine nuances. Clearly, then, the theologian need not be disturbed by the suggestion that his science is untrustworthy simply because it is couched in a particular language and has developed in a certain historical and cultural context. The universal claims of any science are always hedged by the qualification: capable of being understood and tested by anyone who troubles to learn the language and procedures of the science.

Moreover because meaning, operationally understood, is the way people use signs, it would be naïve to look upon our grammars and dictionaries as anything but shrines that stand in need of constant remodeling if they are to house the living reality of language. It is this state of continual flux that is ruinous for our ideals of order. Try as we may, we cannot eliminate the ambiguities and vagaries of usage which prevent language from functioning "logically" (mechanically). An element of semantic vagueness is inevitable so long as the different levels of meaning interact and necessitate our coming to terms with the untidy "implications of utterance" of which Firth has spoken.[7] Apparently it was the recognition of this amorphousness that transformed the confident Wittgenstein of the *Tractatus* into the Socratic seeker of the *Investigations*. Language is not one game—"One might say that the concept 'game' is a concept with blurred edges"[8]—but several families of interrelated games.

There is comfort in this linguistic realism for the theologian who has been harried by the dialogue-paralyzing question: "What do you mean?" Regrettably, an egocentric stipulation is frequently attached to this question, so that the success of the theologian's communication is adjudged

7. "Modes of Meaning" in *Preliminary Reports for the Seventh Linguistic Congress* (London, 1952), cited by Crystal, *Linguistics, Language and Religion* (London, Burns & Oates, 1965), p. 102.

8. *Philosophical Investigations,* Eng. trans. G. E. M. Anscombe (New York, Macmillan, 1957), §71.

by a rigid norm of truth, by a cut-and-dried "logic of language" that makes any reference to a nonempirical or not-directly empirical experience an unpardonable solecism. There are complications, to be sure, that are proper to theological and religious discourse, not the least of which is that the trained specialist, unlike his counterpart in other academic disciplines, must still listen to the Christian people of God whose understanding of the revealed Word may grow or be enriched because they are not just uttering it but living it as a way of life. But these difficulties ought rather to prove a challenge to the theologian's sense of precision than a capitulation to the egocentricity that blights many contemporary analyses. The suggestion that all usage but the speaker's is to be rejected lacks the tolerant flexibility of the trained linguist who has warned us that

> textbooks are only guides to language, and should not be confused with the living language itself; aesthetic judgements vary considerably from person to person, and are no basis for supposedly objective linguistic statements; logic and language . . . do not mix; analogical deduction has no foundation because of the uniqueness of each language's structure; and writing has no superiority over speech, from which it is derived, and which has a status and principles all its own.[9]

With these cautions in mind, let us turn to the current forms of linguistic analysis as they are applied to religious discourse. For the sake of simplicity and brevity, we have chosen the key term of religious language, "God," as the focal point for our discussion.

The basic questions about "God" that expose the main lines of logical investigation are: What does 'God' mean? What rules of logic govern the theologian's statements about God and the inferences he draws from them? Practically, the first question belongs to an apologetic perspec-

9. Crystal, *Linguistics*, pp. 114–15.

tive and is in fact preliminary to the crucial issue of justification; the second more properly concerns the believer interested in, or querulous of, theological methodology. It is generally acknowledged that comparatively little has been written about the latter topic, whereas the former has been wrung dry by philosophers of every persuasion. In this chapter, in keeping with the general tenor of this work, neither question will be discussed intensively. We are interested in presuppositions, in the frames of reference that so to speak formulate these questions and define the range of their anticipated anwers. An understanding of these undoubtedly can help the theologian "show the fly the way out of the fly-bottle." How else is he to learn what these questions really mean and what resources he must tap to answer them?

As far as we can judge, there is nothing peculiar or bizarre about the educational psychology of religious people. In the West, children and converts are taught who the Christian or Jewish God is from Scriptural accounts; they learn to affirm certain things about him in formal credal statements; they are urged to nourish these beliefs by prayer and other ritualistic exercises of piety. Plainly the goal of this teaching is to form the student to how the world is, which as we know means that he must be taught an outlook or a group of attitudes that comprise a scheme of values. As in any other field of indoctrination, religious education is unsuccessful to the degree that its student does not understand, does not self-appropriate. Hence we are likely to be told that this process climaxes in experience. Unless one is brought to the fullest possible realization of his beliefs and worship, he really does not experience God as a person. He may know "facts" about God but he does not live that religious life which alone makes God truly meaningful.

If this description of the course of religious education is accurate, then its implications cannot be ignored in subsequent theological reflection. The guiding supposition,

borne out by everyday life, is that our spontaneous, unreflected concepts veer naturally in the direction of reflected
scientific or communicable concepts. As Vygotsky and other
psychologists who have studied children inform us, autistic
thinking must become scientific: it must be explicitly fitted
into a system if a child is to learn to communicate. Therefore the critical question about the meaning of God, viewed
systematically, consists in examining its sustaining contexts,
both immediate and remote. This investigation undoubtedly forms an integral part of maturing religious thought.

In the Western biblical and Koranic traditions, the
remote context encompasses an inaugural vision or a series
of manifestations of the Sacred, in which the divine name
is revealed, and through which the divine mission of the
prophet or teacher is authenticated. For the listener this
authentication requires signs, oftentimes cosmic events,
which are indices of divine power or presence. As master
of Nature, God is the one who has performed the cosmogonic act and certain other deeds, so that only "the fool"
who cannot "look and see" would dare deny his existence.
An originating "experience" has thus come to determine
how one is to experience the world, and a series of meaningful propositions is gradually formulated that evince his
cosmological perspective. This perspective on reality that
follows the normal course of scientific reflection is con-
tinually reenforced by reasonings which inevitably raise
paradoxes and further difficulties because these reasonings
rest upon foundations which in turn they justify. Since we
are caught in this series of concentric circles, one must risk
being branded irrational or heretical if he is to break out
of the structure in order to question it. Granted that this
questioning has often arisen in reaction to an immediate
context (Sartre's *The Words* exemplifies how his atheism
was stimulated by a distaste for the traditions, practices, and
bourgeois values that encrusted his childhood exposure to
Christianity); still it clearly illustrates the basic problem

of all religious questioning. For if we pose the question, "What does 'God' mean?" the religious person rightfully insists that it can only be answered within his context of experience. How, then, is the questioner to ask about meaning if what he really is probing is the structure of meaning itself? He cannot participate in dialogue unless he stands within the believer's context, nor can he ruthlessly yet sympathetically examine the religious structure of meaning unless he plants himself firmly on the outside.

The religious apologete sounds suspiciouly defensive if he begins his retort with the remark that this dilemma is not unique to the religious situation. What "believer" after all, whether in science or in any other popular scheme, can escape the ultimate reflective paradox of his commitment? Was not this Hegel's point in meditating supposition and presupposition, the shorthand notation for the truism that the immediate is not in itself intelligible and that the intelligible is not in itself immediate? Just because we have become accustomed to our modes of thought to the degree that we no longer recognize them as patterns, we cannot in critical reflection ignore the complexity of observation and tumble back into the naïve realism which makes an unsophisticated empiricism so philosophically attractive. And yet this is precisely what many partisans of analytic technique appear to do—a move that inevitably confuses the issues of language analysis with the epistemology and metaphysics of empiricism. We find ourselves willy-nilly going back over the same ground, notwithstanding an expressed aversion to metaphysics, if only because the good sense of these philosophers will not permit them to ignore completely language's nonlinguistic reference. Max Black, for instance, in an otherwise sensitive treatment of scientific models and archetypes, has rightfully called attention to the inherent dangers of the process of *Vorstellen*. But even if we do run the risk of turning our imaginative models into straitjackets or self-certifying myths, must we believe that the requirements of systematic or metaphysical thought permanently insulate us from "empirical disproof"? It would seem to be the way of all theorizing to try to harmonize any notes that sound discordant, at least to the point where it becomes imperative to change the melody. Yet Black insinuates that the empirical corrective is pellucid, as if this too were not model become myth, the imaginative element of science become dogma. It was not to his interest to have questioned empiricism's world-experience-truth-proof schema.[10] Had he done so, would he have not found himself trapped in "metaphysical" language because of having to deal with the illusive assumptions of thought that are of the essence of questioning? Could he have been so sure that there are no roads from grammar to metaphysics?

Without repeating our earlier discussion of empiricism, perhaps it is not an oversimplification for us to regard these differences of analytic mentality as springing from opposing estimates concerning the presuppositions of thought. Black has responded to those who seek an ultimate ground or reason for linguistic rules that in the last analysis they must fall back on pragmatic considerations of convenience and usefulness. This is all the justification that can reasonably be demanded. Religious thinkers, on the other hand, are forced into metaphysical reasoning by the holistic nature of religious experience. Consequently, they find it congenial to emphasize that question-asking presumes the existence of an intelligible "Real," that the truth revealed to us is a multi-leveled concept (what we know, for instance, is true, but we do not believe that we have exhausted Truth), that experience—our way of testing out and becoming adept at handling the world insofar as it touches us—is by definition an abstraction from the totality of the Real. Moreover, although we may like to think of our experience as something personal or proper to ourselves as individuals,

10. *Models and Metaphors: Studies in Language and Philosophy* (Ithaca, N.Y., Cornell University Press, 1962), p. 242.

religious thinkers note that we are compelled to describe or communicate it by a further abstraction, language, that communal element which in many instances seems to hang rather loosely about our consciousness. Hence it can scarcely be mere chance that the etymological roots of "conscious," "conscience," and their cognates suggest a solidarity in knowledge. For it is this "togetherness" of consciousness that we stressed when we depicted truth as a dialogue, since verification of any kind—religious, mathematical, or scientific—is meaningful only to participants in a kind of conversation. Thus the revelation to the Hebrews took place within the context of a covenant and in concepts familiar to that people, a fact that has encouraged some theologians to explain prophetic inspiration "from within," that is, as a privileged witnessing to, for, and of a "collective consciousness." In his own way, has not Max Black made a similar appeal by resorting to the "pragmatic considerations of convenience and usefulness"?

Once it has become clear that the question of the meaning of 'God' has to be posed within designated cultural limits, we are ready to face two further complications. First, it is readily acknowledged that there was a development within this Hebraic "collective consciousness." God for Isaiah or the Wisdom authors was not merely the Yahweh of the Mosaic hierophanies. Second, having won the concession that an unqualified "What does 'God' mean?" is practically meaningless, the theologian must still elaborate his specific concept of God or gods in relation to the designations of other cultures. Heretofore, the Western philosophical tradition has offered no scope for the discussion of these issues because investigating the meaning of 'God' has in practice been reduced to the question of proving His existence to atheists and agnostics. Human consciousness was exploited in the hope of uncovering a religious a priori of sorts, for do not the "possibilities of experiencing" and the thrust toward system and total grasp lay bare the root of man's religious interpretation of the world? In this respect, Paul Tillich's Ultimate Concern is of a piece with the argumentation of St. Thomas Aquinas, whose celebrated proofs conclude that the ultimate ground upon which rational thought is built is "what we mean by 'God.' "

It is always dangerous to generalize, but can we not say that our difficulties with these arguments, which have comprised the traditional fare of the philosophy of religion, are less with their matter than with their form? Assuredly there will always be some interest in their internal logic and, more broadly conceived, in the logical procedure of theologians. And in the foreseeable future, we will undoubtedly continue to weigh these arguments against the epistemological objections of empiricism. But our predicament is that in every discussion concerning them we revert to the question of how an Ultimate Concern, Prime Mover, First Cause, and the like can be what we mean by 'God.' As a rationalization or justification of a commitment, they carry the conviction of a personal God. But if we do not already see the world theistically, will these cosmological proofs persuade us?

We have already noted that in the current discussion of the structure of argument it is impossible to omit references to formative patterns or conceptual *Gestalten*. This explains the philosophical interest in the process of education insofar as teaching provides us with these requisite anticipatory schemes for knowledge, as well as with the tools of reflection for criticizing them. But, nothwithstanding our critical advances, the mirage of unbiased, objective thought still deludes us. We pursue beginnings, unmindful of the nature of our reflection (which by definition precludes the idea of mind as a *tabula rasa*), hopeful of capturing the phantom origins of religion and language. By a kind of retrojection to the primitive, we suppose we will find an absolute ground that will explain rationality once and for all, even though ethnologists and anthropologists have exploded the idea of a society or people without a complex religious and linguistic structure.

The merit of reminding ourselves of our folly is that it should diminish any unrealistic expectations we may still entertain about the suasive power of apologetic arguments. At the same time, we are coerced into taking another hard look at "experience," a notion whose very elasticity has brought it into considerable philosophical disrepute. Granted that in any circumstance this term is hard to make precise, especially in the broad sense in which we use it as synonymous with an interpretation based upon one's whole attitude toward life; still we cannot do without it in any adequate discussion of meaning. The difficulty of being exact is compounded when we begin to talk about religious experience, particularly if we imply that we intend to designate something on a par with aesthetic, unusual, rewarding, traumatic, or historical experience. Regrettably by suggesting that religious experience is just another kind of particular experiencing, we may insinuate the falsehood that every authentically religious person is a mystic, enjoying either an immediate intuition of, or a direct contact with, "the Divine." On the other hand, no committed believer can accept the idea that religious experience even taken *in globo* is properly understood as any total reaction to life or as the communal celebration of a community's interpersonal relations.[11]

11. Williams James' *The Varieties of Religious Experience* (New York, Random House, Modern Library, 1902), has rightfully been criticized as narrowly subjective. Here I have in mind writers like Georg Simmel in his *Lebensanschauung* (München, Duncker & Humblot, 1922), and his "Contribution to the Sociology of Religion," *American Journal of Sociology, 11* (1905), 359 ff., or John Macmurray, in *The Structure of Religious Experience* (New Haven, Yale University Press, 1936), and in his two volumes of Gifford Lectures: *The Self as Agent* and *Persons in Relations* (London, Faber & Faber, 1957).

As a result of his apparent fudging, the believer readily finds himself in an unenviable defensive position. What he means by "religious experience" may also involve the dimension of being-in-the-Church, that is, an experience in harmony with certain dogmas or popular beliefs. If he is Christian, he will want to insist on a relationship to Christ, although part of his description might include a reaction similar to that of Paul Claudel at the moment when he suddenly heard the music in the cathedral of Notre Dame. If he is pressed to generalize this understanding in order to include other religions, the believer is apt to fall back on the definitions of Otto or Eliade, who characterize this experience as a relationship to "the Holy," "the Sacred," or "the Transcendent" (a supernatural being or beings). Obviously, none of these terms, when pursued with Wittgensteinian fervor, can stand up very long without a renewed appeal to experience. It then becomes easy to label religious statements nonsense, and to point out the contradiction involved in credal affirmations and purportedly communicable propositions made about a wholly transcendent or unutterable deity. But we must in all honesty take our Wittgenstein undiluted. Is not ostensive definition itself confusingly ambiguous? Does not any exercise of criticism, unhinged from the experiential context inspiring it, gambol on the edge of self-defeat and intellectual suicide? "The confusions which occupy us arise when language is like an engine idling, not when it is doing work."

These remarks on experience give point to the adage that without common grounds there can be no dispute. However, the impression is frequently created that for the sake of argument terminological difficulties have been waived. We now stand within the theologian's experiential context where we will examine his meaning and scrutinize his logic. Presumably it is immaterial whether or not the same empiricist principles are applied, although one would surmise that their application would swiftly lead to an impasse.[12]

A standard form of this philosophical critique is to study the predicates most commonly used of God (or gods): 'father,' 'good,' 'just,' 'crucified' (Paul Ziff has called these the predicates with unproblematic conditions because they are readily satisfied or satisfiable by someone or something),[13] 'omniscient,' 'omnipotent,' or 'eternal' (Ziff's predicates of problematic conditions; basically a question of whether these predicates are intelligible or not). Let us briefly consider one of these latter predicates, 'omnipotence,' since it offers us a suitable paradigm case and continues to be, astonishingly, a fertile field of philosophical discussion.[14] The obvious difficulty is to state precisely what this concept means, for if God can do absolutely anything, we shift automatically to the problem of evil; if He can do only what He can do, we have no time for empty tautology; and, if He can do only certain things, then He must be finite. For this reason, Charles Hartshorne has defended a White-headian divine relativity,[15] whereas Barthian theologians are thereby convinced of the absolute futility of a philosophical approach to God.

The current trend among philosophers who wish to be noncommittal in this anti-metaphysical age is to emphasize the linguistic contexts of words like 'omnipotent' and

12. A classic example of this technique is Ronald W. Hepburn's *Christianity and Paradox: Critical Studies in Twentieth-Century Theology* (London, Watts, 1958).

13. "About God" in *Religious Experience and Truth*, pp. 198 ff.

14. I am indebted to Paul G. Kuntz for a three-page selective bibliography on this topic attached to his working paper: "The Sense and Nonsense of Omnipotence: Philosophic Reflections on the Text 'With God All Things Are Possible,' "—a paper stimulated by Robert C. Coburn's "Omniscience and Omnipotence," read at the University of Chicago, May 4, 1965.

15. See *The Divine Relativity* (New Haven, Yale University Press, 1948); his controversy with John Wild in *The Review of Metaphysics*, 2 (1948), and 4 (1950); and his recent discussion in *The Logic of Perfection and Other Essays in Neoclassical Metaphysics* (LaSalle, Illinois, The Open Court, 1962).

'eternal.' Essentially, this was the recommendation of William James when he remarked that we ought to see these titles as products of theological professionalism, and before him of Thomas Hobbes, who suggested that they be treated as pious effusions. Because, they said, the religious attitude is one of self-effacement, deference, and unquestioning reverence, the religious person naturally magnifies the divine characteristics, particularly in a situation of prayerful petition. Thus in the days of powerful monarchs, it was appropriate to apply the honorifics of king or emperor to the divine majesty, if for no other reason than that the king was God's vice-gerent. But these explanations, psychologically or linguistically informative as they may be, do not come to grips with the fundamental issue: the charge of anthropomorphism that has been leveled against religious discourse since the time of Xenophanes. The "negative theology" of the Pseudo-Denis represents an attempt to cope with this problem, one that in the medieval period called forth Aquinas' more comprehensive and nuanced doctrine of analogy, which Father Bochenski has recently updated as a theory of the formal properties of relations.

The former Oxford theologian (currently Bishop of Durham) Ian Ramsey, in view of the concentrated empiricist atmosphere in which he writes, sidesteps the metaphysical implications of analogy but has tried to show that the disclosure-function of religious language is not odd. On the contrary, the peculiarity of much of human discourse, in the natural sciences, mathematics, sociology, and psychology, is its dependence upon models and metaphors which enable us to be articulate in complex logical situations.[16] From another viewpoint, therefore, Ramsey's

16. In his *Models and Mystery* (London, Oxford University Press, 1964), Ramsey has developed themes of the earlier *Religious Language* by drawing heavily upon Max Black, *Models and Metaphors,* and B. H. Kazemier and D. Vuysje, eds., *The Concept and the Role of the Model in Mathematics and Natural and Social Sciences* (Utrecht, D. Riedel, 1961).

discussion confirms the analysis of symbols and myth of the preceding chapter. He has seen clearly that the inherent anthropomorphism of our thought and expression is rooted in our symbolic nature. Consequently, his proposal of models—like the scholastic theory of the phantasm, the Kantian notion of the Transcendental Imagination, or the Hegelian process of *Vorstellen*—was conceived as an alternate mode of bridging the gap between immediate sense experience and theoretical speculation. "It might be said that either we permit picturing models or take refuge in the inexpressible, unless perhaps we sponsor a Scholastic doctrine of analogy."[17]

That we think is obvious. But how we think, traditionally explained as a movement out of (generalization), and finally back into (verification), sense experience, still awaits definitive clarification. It is this elusive process, in which all the key logical and epistemological terms figure prominently—'meaning,' 'truth,' 'evidence,' 'proof,' etc.—that either a theory of analogy, or Wittgenstein's picturing, or Ramsey's modeling, presumably explicates. Yet the security of an absolute, universally accepted elucidation constantly eludes us. This in itself should warn us again that we are operating within a context that regulates the criteria of valid thought. And so, how we evaluate our anthropomorphizing rests ultimately upon the fundamental image we entertain of ourselves as men. In a Cartesian "mentalism," God must be clearly and distinctly represented uncontaminated by any suggestion of the corporeal, mechanical automaton. In the variegated forms of empiricism, sensism, and materialism, God can only be spoken of in the vague spiritual terms of deism or agnosticism. Evidently, commencing from these opposing starting-points, we can scarcely have ears attuned to, not to say sympathetic toward, customary religious language.

17. *Models and Mystery*, p. 7.

There is a style of contemporary thought that makes it possible for us to accept anthropomorphism more graciously. If we stop looking at the body as a thing and forget the resultant talk of modern philosophy about the senses, then the door is open to "the body" as a medium or situator: to what permits us to be located in and present to "a world." Personalists are wont to stress that it is through his body that another is physically present to us, rendered apt, that is, for the authentically human act of presence which is a communicating with a view to communion. Even in the traditional philosophy of man, it was recognized that hearing, touch, and sight are formless capacities; they must be educated if they are to serve us in the milieu from which, in which, and for which we exist. The importance of this notion is not merely that it emphasizes the significant role of "the group" or society in forming the discriminations of intelligent communication ("others" are essential to our becoming and being men), but it also invites further reflection on the representative character of thought (the conventional vocabulary of epistemology is replete with terms like 'idea,' 'image,' and 'copy') as grounded in its initial presentative aspect. Heinz Werner has argued from genetic psychology that these presentations lack the clearcut distinction of thought from perception, emotion, and motor action. Thought itself is this discriminating function, the representing activity that is essentially interpretative. Thus in cultures less complicated than our own there was a relatively limited differentiation of object and subject, of perception and feeling, of idea and action; in brief, one detects a greater continuity of man with his world than in our self-consciously scientific age. Werner's suggestion is that in this deeper immersion in the concrete, which accounts for the characteristics of "primitive" thought— its diffuse, holophrastic conceptualization and its apparent tolerance of inconsistency—lie the roots of anthropomorphism.

In its primordial form—contrary to what it later becomes—anthropomorphism is magically conditioned "naturalization" of the personality. In order to overcome nature, man, as it were, to some degree transforms himself into nature. He *becomes* nature by virtue of a unity of inner being and outer attitude.[18]

Any number of examples come spontaneously to mind: the rituals of rainmaking ceremonies, of fertility rites, of totemism, even such things as the "bear ceremonialism," which undoubtedly is connected with the magic and mythology of the hunt. But rather than flatter ourselves with the questionable supposition that primitives were incapable of transcending the imaginative by a discriminating thrust toward objective thought—indeed, demythologizing is intrinsic to all thought, and Werner does not hesitate to admit that the "primitive moment" is essential to all "higher" functioning—we ought to radicate man's universalizing tendency, and therefore his modeling and anthropomorphism, in the conviction of the universe as nature, that is, as a unified totality. Granted that many of our difficulties over anthropomorphism stem from the fact that we are compelled to convey particular meanings in generalized terms and we know little of the actual process of transition from concrete abstraction to generalization in its true sense; still, the fundamental problem would appear to be a rejection of the thesis of continuity embodied in Augustine's idea of the world—of man preeminently—as the *imago Dei.* To be sure, Bishop Robinson would have us believe that Christians have too long accepted a naïve triple-deckered world and God the Father as an old man with flowing white beard. But he never seems to get beyond these picturings in order to query whether it is feasible to discuss Christianity outside of its proper context of meaning, or whether, in

18. *Comparative Psychology of Mental Development* (New York, Science Editions, Inc., 1961), p. 353.

fact, any system of truth can be significant to one who deliberately stands apart from or in opposition to the group experience of its adherents. It may be fashionable, of course, to assert that the modern mind will not tolerate the religious person's view of himself at home in the world. But if that is the case, how are we to explain the unprecedented popularity of existentialism, of the French magazine *Planète,* and of the works of Teilhard de Chardin, through all of which reverberates the common nostalgia for the earth, for a natural world where man can once again find himself at home? Is it not as true to say that anthropomorphism became intellectually disreputable in the West when man lost himself after the "death of God"?

Throughout this chapter we have seen that the complexities of meaning inevitably involve us in a situation, so that an attempt to talk about 'meaning' divorced from a context, as Wittgenstein himself recognized, is fruitless. Yet our quest for certitude is normally not satisfied with this kind of answer. We want to push farther and ground ourselves on the bedrock of absolute truth. "How," we ask, "does one justify a context? Is there a scientific method for substantiating one's view of the world?" Paradoxically, we appear caught up in a vicious circle, and we lack Hegel's courage to face a surd at the beginning of our philosophizing.

Admittedly, there is no absolute, once-and-for-all resolution of this problem. Our expectancy will always lead us to uncover data, which, in turn, serve to fortify our anticipations. But it is an oversimplification to picture our predicament in a way that blanches all discrepancies and rules out the phenomenon of growth. For we know that our intellectual structures are not stagnant and the data they illuminate are not necessarily sifted to a fine consistency. In a word, we grow by the assimilation–accommodation process Piaget has described, that is, by correcting our viewpoints through an uninterrupted dialogue.

To some believers this epistemology appears suspect if not blatantly false. For them it is not enough to describe the rationale of Christianity as one that accounts for all the data to be harmonized: the fact of belief, the events of the Old and New Testaments, one's day-to-day experience of hope and charity and sinfulness and forgiveness. They want an infallible apologetic: one that compels every truly rational man to truth and convicts every unbeliever or dissenter of irrationality or malice. The desire for this kind of assurance is understandable. But it is questionable whether the data of contemporary philosophy and psychology will establish their kind of philosophical realism, and whether their talk about philosophical truth leaves room for the essential freedom of the act of faith. In the long run, does not a confrontation with other, non-Christian traditions require us to admit frankly that one's Christianity is a commitment, and that a resultant philosophy is merely a way of rationalizing or making sense out of lived experience?

In the following chapter we shall focus our attention upon this act of choice by surveying some of the philosophico-religious problems that arise in an intellectual reflection upon the history of religions.

SEVEN. THE HISTORY AND PHENOMENOLOGY OF RELIGION

> A religious symbol not only reveals a pattern
> of reality or a dimension of existence, it
> brings at the same time a *meaning to human
> existence.*
>
> ELIADE, *Mephistopheles and the Androgyne*

At the beginning of this book we remarked that many of the problems of the contemporary Western-oriented Christian theologian stem from the prodigious "information explosion" of the past quarter-century. Not only has the theology of the West itself grown like Topsy—the influence of historical discoveries upon the biblical movement and upon patristic, conciliar, and moral (e.g. contraception) studies comes immediately to mind—but its involvement with hermeneutics has drawn it into the vortex of contemporary philosophy, and both its concern for the nonbeliever and its ecumenical reach have compelled an investigation of the religious phenomenon particularly as it has displayed itself outside of Christianity. Theologians have prudently relied on the historians of religions for this data, although they have tended to be skeptical about observations handed to them wrapped in speculative constructions, principally regarding origins. Yet it would be foolish to suppose that nothing has happened in *Religionswissenschaft* since Müller, Tylor, Frazer, Schmidt, or Otto, as if the sentiment against categorizing were never felt in this discipline. The reality, consisting in a wealth of materials wellnigh overwhelming, has actually prompted the

cry of despair: "What are we to make out of all of this data?"
As Eliade has told us even of "primitives":

> The religious life appears complex even at the most
> archaic stages of culture. Among the peoples still in the
> stage of food-gathering and hunting small animals
> (Australians, Pygmies, Fuegians, etc.), the belief in a
> Supreme Being or "Lord of the Animals" is inter-
> mingled with beliefs in culture-heroes and mythical
> ancestors; prayers and offerings to the gods coexist with
> totemic practices, the cult of the dead, and hunting and
> fertility magic. The morphology of religious experi-
> ence is also of a surprising richness. One has only to
> consider the experiences set in motion by the puberty
> initiation or by various seasonal ceremonies and es-
> pecially the experiences of medicine men and shamans.
> The latter constitute the religious and cultural elite of
> any primitive society; phenomenologically their experi-
> encies may be likened to those of the mystics of more ad-
> vanced cultures—a comparison which alone is enough
> to destroy any hypothesis of simplicity and homo-
> geneity in primitive religious life.[1]

This warning against hasty generalization ought not to
be interpreted as an antisystematic bias. The work of the
historian of religions as an intellectual enterprise will always
be one of systematic ordering, even though today's scholar
senses the danger of reductionism implicit in global sche-
matizations. Yet there is a danger that scholarly caution
can obfuscate the issue for the nonspecialist, particularly
for the interested observer who has doubts about the relevance of the historian of religions' project. In fact, even
the accredited scientists of this field appear to be uncertain
about their purpose and so also about methodology. For is

1. "Structures and Changes in the History of Religion," in *City Invincible: A Symposium on Urbanization and Cultural Development in the
Ancient Near East* (Chicago, University of Chicago Press, 1960), p. 351.

the goal to be a sort of specialized historian, one who sets before us a cluster of positivist-flavored facts: details of initiation and sacrifice rituals, of divine genealogies, and so forth? Van der Leeuw, in spite of the fact that he has usurped the term phenomenology, apparently has so envisioned his task that it runs the risk of having to justify itself solely on the grounds of "knowledge for knowledge's sake." It is clear that the Dutch scholar felt that the research of his descriptions was its own reward. Besides, he wanted to avoid the imputation of being an Hegelian or Tylorean, since presumably that meant a commitment to an inexorable law of progress that unaccountably discontinued with one's own religion or upon reaching the apogee of Christianity. A more rigorous form of Husserlian phenomenology has been advocated by Ernst Benz and Mircea Eliade, who hope to clarify the contemporary religious consciousness by extricating its latent "tradition of earlier forms of religious experiences and of earlier stages of religious consciousness. . . . Somewhere in the bedrock layer of our religious awareness, the religious experience and various conceptual forms of our primitive forefathers live on."[2] This is not, be it noted, a purely psychoanalytic program, but a view of "history," "meaning," and "truth" (argued vigorously by Paul Ricoeur in *History and Truth*[3]) that transforms a dead past into a present revelation.

It would be unrealistic to suppose that there is no dovetailing of these divergent interests or emphases, and we were rather invidiously to juxtapose the studies of anthropologists like Professor Elkin and Mr. Godfrey Lienhardt to the more theoretical work of Adolf Jensen, or to insist that Eliade's construction is "subjective" whereas Zaehner's is

---

2. Ernst Benz, "On Understanding Non-Christian Religions," in Mircea Eliade and Joseph Kitagawa, eds., *The History of Religions: Essays in Methodology* (Chicago, The University of Chicago Press, 1959), p. 130.

3. Paul Ricoeur, *History and Truth*, Eng. trans. Charles A. Kelbley (Evanston, Northwestern University Press, 1965), pp. 21–40.

"objective." There is, indeed, always the imminent temptation to confuse differences of temperament with standards
of objectivity, with the result that the really fundamental
point of divergence becomes blurred. It should be noted
that all investigators of religious phenomena, whether their
philosophical inclinations be in the direction of positivism
or phenomenology, have to begin with fairly clear ideas
about what they are researching, even though an anthropologist might not be concerned to offer anything but a
pragmatic answer to the basic theological question: "What
is a 'religious fact'?" Lienhardt, for instance, replied to this
query: "I really don't know"; by which he meant, presumably, that one simply cannot isolate an attitude toward life
and describe it as if it were another empirical element or
component.[4] The anthropological observer inquires into a
people's history, traditions, and beliefs and describes conduct that we are inclined to call religious: attitudes toward
the deity or deities, the dead and spirits, beliefs touching
man and his destiny, sacrifice and rituals, and so forth. His
interest, then, is not to controvert Freud's theory of the
totemic origin of religion (although Claude Lévi-Strauss has
done so because he rejects out of hand the concept of totemism).[5] Rather it is to show us, as Elkin has, how totemism
functions concretely in regulating marriages and is in the
last analysis a manner of seeing the world that colors the
social groupings of Australian aborigines, has inspired their
mythologies and ceremonies, and links them with their past.
In our society, in which religion has become largely a matter
of belief in God, we require a succinct definition, if only
because the reporter or commentator on religion must say
something to distinguish the scoffer, agnostic, or similarly
minded skeptic who may share other facets of our lives. To
the contrary, the anthropologist reporting on the Nuer or
Dinka or Bororo need not mention disbelievers. In fact he

4. In a lecture given at the University of Chicago, May 4, 1966.
5. *The Australian Aborigines* (Garden City, N.Y., Doubleday, 1964).

cannot—because the entire local tribal organization, as in the typical case of the Australian aborigines, is bound up with kinship-grouping, mythological history, the pre-existence of spirits, and totemism, as well as with economics. To talk about the religion of these peoples is to talk about life as it is governed by a complete set of values. Yet because we who have been exposed to a secularist environment are reluctant to equate religion with any total view of reality, we are inclined to sift this historical and anthropological data in an attempt to shake out a specifically religion-constituting characteristic. Initially, therefore, we are satisfied when Lowie tells us, along with Marett and Goldenweiser, that religion is constituted by supernaturalism,[6] or, in Otto's terms, by "the holy," or, to follow Eliade, defined by the dimensions of the Sacred.

However useful and necessary these words may be for descriptive purposes, it is evident that they are usually defined within a closed system: "holy" means "sacred," which means "supernatural," which means "transcendent." Unfortunately, the only other convenient way of mapping them is by reference to their dialectical antipodes: "natural," "ordinary," "profane," and the like. "Religion," Lowie once wrote, "is verily a universal feature of human culture, not because all societies foster a belief in spirits, but because all recognize in some form or other awe-inspiring, extraordinary manifestations of reality."[7] Undoubtedly this is a legitimate observation for an anthropologist who has in mind either his own dealings with, or descriptive materials about, the Crow, the Bukaua, or Polynesian groups. But it will not do for the sophisticated secularist critic who recognizes that the Sacred and Profane subtly interpenetrate in an elusive dialectic and who in addition is not privy to that all-important experience which would permit him to in-

6. Robert H. Lowie, *Primitive Religion* (New York, Grosset & Dunlap, 1952), p. xvi.
7. Ibid.

terpret certain extraordinary phenomena as divine. Not that he is unwilling to call some of his own experiences extraordinary—in keeping with common usage—but he does not share the suppositions which allow him to classify these as anything but unusual or currently inexplicable.

The thrust of Mircea Eliade's thought (like that of Erich Heller in the area of literature and philosophy) would appear to be directed toward restoring this rupture of communication. Building upon his detailed historical studies, which bolster Lowie's assertion of a universal recognition of the extraordinary, Eliade is interested in composing the "Patterns in Comparative Religion" with the intent of exhibiting homologies. This, of course, is the decisive step of a Husserlian-type phenomenology, for Eliade argues that these similarities manifest the essential structures of human consciousness. Why, then, do some of our contemporaries refuse their past and insist that some of these allegedly active structures are merely historical remnants of bygone, primitive ages? Because, Eliade replies, in an a- or anti-historical frenzy they have repressed their mythic consciousness to subconscious realms. That they have done violence to the archetypes of the human spirit is evidenced by our literature and philosophy, where a pervasive existential *Angst* and the despair of meaninglessness betray themselves, along with a childish, ephemeral striving to kill time and to live the moment by plunging into it and flying from all that constitutes it as a moment.

To elaborate on this indictment of the modern mind is not to our purpose: it would entail an expanded rehearsal of the philosophical themes we have already discussed in previous chapters. The fundamental philosophic issue is that of the morality of knowledge. For if truth is a value, it follows that the values of the intellect should also, at some time or other, come under careful scrutiny. After all, the Enlightenment legacy of an unrestricted right to know and its accompanying myth of endless progress, which Erich

Heller has depicted as responsible for the transmogrification of Faust from a desperate sinner to a tragic hero,[8] have been depreciated by the Pandora's box of doubts and uncertainties about thought opened by both Hegelians and Wittgensteinians. Perhaps the Bomb has succeeded where nothing else has in putting an end to our escapades of irresponsible inquiry.

For the uninitiated the complexities of Eliade's discussion are due in large measure to the sheer intractability or stubborn intransigence of his material. We have already noted that the social anthropologists describe religions in their variegated contexts. R. C. Zaehner has remarked that philosophy has never been divorced from religion in India; all sects and schools of post-Vedic Hinduism accept as a self-evident fact the doctrine of the transmigration of souls, its resultant law of *karma,* and the all-embracing *dharma* of the universe.[9] And so, although we might inaugurate our investigation of religion in pursuit of "theological" data (understood in the loose sense of what appertains to God, deities, or the divine), we soon find ourselves inveigled into unraveling at times intricate cosmological and anthropological schemes. Moreover, it is now impossible either to suppose that religions develop in a unilinear fashion or to ignore the fractional groupings within a religious family. Ninian Smart, for instance, has distinguished within the Hindu–Buddhist tradition the agnostic–atheistic pluralism of Jainism and perhaps of the *Theravāda* from the transtheistic monism of the *Advaita Vedānta* and the transmonistic theism of Rāmānuja.[10] Similarly, W. K. C. Guthrie has reminded us that Greek religion embodied conflicting

8. "Faust's Damnation: The Morality of Knowledge," in *The Artist's Journey into the Interior and Other Essays* (New York, Random House, 1965), pp. 3–44.

9. R. C. Zaehner, *Hinduism* (London, Oxford University Press, 1962), pp. 5, 178.

10. S. G. F. Brandon, ed., *The Saviour God* (Manchester, Manchester University Press, 1963), p. 167.

140   *Reflective Theology*

tendencies: one which emphasized the gulf between man
and god (and therefore man's hubris in trying to bridge it)
and another which stressed the kinship of the human and the
divine.[11] Neither can we minimize other variants of the
god–man–world relationship over the course of centuries.
The apparent indifference of Egyptian thinkers to man's
creation, a general tendency in Indian religions to ignore
the world, an evanescence of high gods into otiose deities, a
predominant man–world relationship in Taoism, and a
growing spiritualization of the gods in the later and more
philosophical developments of Greek religion would seem
to recommend not only that we speak more reservedly about
religious languages but that we ought to despair over the
whole project of illuminating the religious structures of
human consciousness.

Yet it would be disastrous to celebrate the analytic at the
expense of the synthetic, as if the philosophers of the past
who have described the trajectory of human intellection as
a movement toward unity (the One or Absolute) had
merely been outraged by a metaphysical incubus. Hence we
cannot honestly dismiss the hardheaded thinking of Kant
(*pace* Bertrand Russell) without replacing it with a careful
examination of the conditions of thought. Kant's triumph
was to have reiterated, in the terminology of the Newtonian
Age of Science, that the limited scope of human thought
involves us in talk about both sides of the border: that the
phenomenal, in other words, can be thought only in terms
of the noumenal, and that the conditions of human understanding require their implementation in the ideals of
Reason. At this juncture it is important that we recall our
native holism because historians of religions have as a rule
acknowledged this thrust toward totality or Ultimate Reality as a constant of the religious consciousness which, even in
the *soi-disant* a-cosmological religions, is accompanied by a

11. *The Greeks and Their Gods* (Boston, Beacon Press, 1962), p. 114.

belief in the divine order of things. Consequently, we are faced with the question: Is human knowledge or science at bottom a religious act? Was Nietzsche right when he lambasted the atheistic scientists of his day:

> But one will have understood what I am driving at: our faith in science still rests upon a metaphysical belief. We, the godless and anti-metaphysical scholars of today, even we, I say, draw our flames from the fire which the belief of a thousand years has enkindled— from that Christian faith which was Plato's too, the belief that God is the truth and that the truth is divine.[12]

Let us approach this problem through the data of the history of religions. In a brief discussion of the mythology of Australian aborigines, Elkin has stated that specific details may be irrelevant or distracting. Our attention should be directed to a myth as a life-giving function: as something that enables "present-day men to walk the path with fidelity, which leads into the sacred dream-time, the source of all life."[13] In its lived awareness, religious thought is never a truncated metaphysical or theological speculation. Its basic stuff is constituted by words and deeds; its sacred rites celebrate the meaning of life symbolically—not just theoretically—by importing us into the fundamental scheme of things: whether immediately into the rhythms of the cosmos, or ultimately into the Unconditioned, the Dharma or Nirvāna, whence Becoming ("impermanence," "suffering," the "not-self") is understood. Throughout the centuries, different forms of life have given birth to, or are reflected in, the different emphases found in our religious traditions. Apparently the Egyptians were little interested in the question of man's origin, and the predominantly ethical character of Taoism is evident: "Man models himself on the earth, the earth on heaven, heaven on the Tao; whilst the Tao models

12. Nietzsche, *The Gay Science*, §344.
13. *Australian Aborigines*, p. 215.

itself on itself as being what it is."[14] But for the most part, our diverse religious traditions are at one in portraying man's present position, and his resultant obligation to "redeem the time" or to "decondition" himself, as due to a rupture of a primordial unity. Because the world exists in a state of "sin"—in a disharmony that is echoed in the "groaning of creation" for its primeval state—man himself must either be redeemed or save himself. Schematically, Thomas Aquinas has drawn a Christian theological picture of this process in his ordering of the *Summa Theologiae*, where the questions on God and the emanations of the Divine Persons are followed in a circular movement by creation and the redemptive work of Christ, so that the virtuous Christian is brought back into the unity of the Father. Among the diverse sects and philosophical schools of Hinduism the notion of the circle figures in the universal image of breaking the fetters or wheel of Time. The idea of "salvation" is predicated upon the assumptions that the universe is governed by cyclic time, that the microcosm (individual soul) is regulated by the same law of cause and effect as the macrocosm, and that escape or liberation *(Moksha* or *mukti)* beyond the changing form of existence (to the Unconditioned) is finally possible for all. In both these schemes, Western and Eastern, we are offered in differently polarizing emphases the basic religious image: a unity embracing God, world, and man, each with its internal tensions and external attractions and repulsions, but bound together in an overarching dialectic or *coincidentia oppositorum* because of their beginning and end.

The interesting feature of these religious constructions is what Godfrey Lienhardt has referred to in the oral rites of the Dinka as the "truth of a situation," that is, not the truth of certain "facts" located in time and space, but "exis-

14. *The Tao Te Ching*, in E. R. Hughes, ed., *Chinese Philosophy in Classical Times* (London, Dent, 1942), p. 153, cited in *Man and His Destiny in the Great Religions*, p. 358.

tential truth": the deeper significance of present events highlighted against the background of the entire sweep of life. Sacrifice, for example, has always been the religious existential act par excellence, for the customary symbolisms of water, woman, blood, and earth transcend their immediate meanings to represent the original and originating acts which produce and sustain human or divinely graced human life. Thus various religions repeat the cosmogonic act, celebrate the deeds of mythical ancestors, or perform rites to ensure the fertility of earth, animal, and man. Christianity's commemorative Eucharist is a similar rite since it recalls or represents the act by which its present participants have the right to bear the dignity of God's children and heirs. The existential character of such acts, therefore, lies in their trans-historicity. Although performed in time, they have eternal significance; although ordinarily addressed to God or divinities, they reveal the true meaning of man; and although they grow out of peculiar contexts, perhaps reflecting different attitudes toward the world because of progressive humanizations of deities, they are never merely human projections because they are "doing what is prescribed."

R. C. Zaehner has noted that the *Purusha-sūkta* combines two elements that are fundamental to the later speculation of the Brāhmanas and Upanishads, namely, that creation is a sacrifice, and that macrocosmic man (the primal man whose dismembered body is the world) is the prototype of microcosmic man. Therefore, "between man and the world there is analogy of being, and since creation is a sacrifice on the macrocosmic scale, so is this sacrifice renewed on the microcosmic scale a creative act which ensures the continued orderly existence of the universe."[15] The importance of this idea cannot be underestimated. It accentuates the basic premise of religious thought—the divine provenance and

15. Zaehner, *Hinduism*, p. 58.

character of reality that enables religious man to have his total views and his analogous language in which to articulate them—and also exposes the nerve of religious reflection that has remained sensitive since Freud's charge of projection. The delicate point of religious reflection is that in it we are always dealing with man's response, with the human speculations, images, and understandings which make it appear that human beings simply create their own situation "as it really is." Thus the skeptic might conclude from Eliade's discussion of the symbolism of the "center"—such items as shamanic ladders, cosmic trees, tethering poles and village layout plans that locate the "center of the universe" and thus mark out a temple or dimension of sacred space— that all there is at stake is a primitive way of man's making himself at home in the world. Yet were this all, we would have to ignore all the data that Eliade has mustered to show that a dialectic of the Sacred and Profane is operative in a centralizing which is not solely the natural activity of bringing to a focus. Assuredly, the symbolism of the "center" preserves the idea of a place of privileged access to God, even though "real" hierophantic centers in which God presumably appeared, like Beth-el, are scarce today and our sanctuaries (aside from a doctrine of the Real Presence) are only replicas of the sites of great theophanies or simply houses of prayer. But the air of nostalgia about our spiritual enterprises and edifices that puts a premium upon spiritual memory—what religion does not hark back to the spiritual giants of yesteryear and idealize the prodigies they worked? —is itself a warning that our strides toward cosmic integration evidenced in our intellectual and cultural attainments are not accompanied by a parallel growth in spiritual experience. In other words, the natural activity of understanding, qua categorizing or unifying, forges links with the world. We control nature by an entering into it that marks our own continuity with it. Man's religious experience, however, is founded upon a rupture of these links.

Homo religiosus discovers himself not just in nature but precisely by breaking out of the repetitions of nature (time) and constituting history (the step back or outside in order to judge time). Seen from man's point of view, this spiritual breaking-through of the Profane, which establishes the sacredness of man, is the existential (in the Heideggerian sense of "making stand out"—*ex-stare*) act of revelation.

Theologians of the Judaeo-Christian-Mohammedan religious tradition particularly insist that the restoration of the world to its true pattern depends upon the divine initiative and the activity of God through the realms of nature, man, and history.[16] Revelation causally defined in this way stands in stark contrast to the conception of those scientists (anthropologists, historians) who of necessity concentrate upon revelation in its effects. An apologetic effort to harmonize these approaches encounters almost insuperable obstacles because in either case, whether one begins "from below" with religious conduct or "from above" with sacred writings and oracles, both sides come together on the middle ground of an inaugurating or authenticating religious experience, which by nature is not susceptible of immediate scientific examination. So far we have seen that the investigable aspect of this experience common to all religious traditions is a complete world view, an outlook that encompasses a unified interpretation of the totality of human experience. But the questions have been raised and are decisive for our times: What is peculiar to the total view of the religious consciousness? What recommends this outlook as more satisfactory than the purview of natural science?

As a rule, theologians have acquired from the controversies of the past a healthy respect for the methods employed in the natural sciences. At the same time, however, thanks to the work of the philosophers of science, they have

16. See, for example, H. Wheeler Robinson's *Inspiration and Revelation in the Old Testament* (London, Oxford University Press, 1962) paperback edition, p. 272; also his *Redemption and Revelation.*

learned to question the principles of interpretation—
materialist, for instance, or empiricist—that constitute the
theoretical explanations of observed phenomena. Fortunately this process of questioning has helped settle the dust
and as a consequence has provoked a deeper probing of the
kind of regularities or patterns that interest, say, physicists,
biologists, and psychologists. The result has been a sharper
focus on our drive or passion for order, whether it be exemplified as in physics by the space–time conception and
the interconnectedness of physical facts manifested by the
complementarity of wave and particle and Pauli's exclusion
principle, or in biology's model of the organism. Obviously,
the contemporary theologian is not competent to challenge
these patterns and modes of experiencing. If anything can
still serve him as an intellectual point of contact with scientists, perhaps this drive for order is still capable of doing
so, even though the supposition of intelligibility undergird-
ing our knowledge schemes has borne the brunt of fierce
philosophical attacks. We have only to recollect the checkered history of proofs for God from Hume to Nietzsche to
appreciate the positivist's recommendation that questions
about an intelligible order or truth are fundamentally
wrongheaded because they are in principle unanswerable.
Yet such a stipulation, I would suggest, dictates fashion, not
law. It cannot decree an end to our self-reflections, to our uncertainties about the validity but especially about the value
of our modes of understanding. Questions of this kind are
addressed to the scientist as a human being; answering them
can clarify for the theologian his basic disagreement with
the naturalistic humanist. The issue can be phrased succinctly: Is "the world" ultimately personal or impersonal?

It might be objected that this is not the issue between the
religious and the secular mind. On the one hand there
are "religious" traditions—the Buddhist, for example—in
which the concept of self or individual has been explicitly
rejected. In fact, the specific contribution of Buddhism to

religious thought has been declared to be its doctrine of non-self—*An-attā* (Pali) or *An-ātman* (Sanskrit): the belief that nothing real corresponds to our ideas of the ego ("I," "mine," "belonging"). Since suffering is regarded as a necessary consequence of being conditioned or impermanent, salvation can only be acquired by a disciplined attention to Reality (the Absolute or Nirvāna), in which the imagined "self" loses its consistency. On the other hand, the Sāṁkhya system of Hinduism admits of no God who might be the personal grounding of the universe. "It is utterly different," Zaehner has pointed out,

> from the dominant pantheistic trend of the Upanishads in that it does not admit an Absolute in which the temporal and the eternal are reconciled, it does not admit the identity in any sense of the individual soul with the Supreme Soul for the very good reason that it denies the existence of the latter, it regards *moksha* not as a merging of the soul into an impersonal Brahman but as its total isolation within its own eternal and timeless essence.[17]

One might attempt to reply to this objection by an appeal to popular religion since the nearly universal phenomenon of personal deities and savior gods seems to attest to a common requirement of the religious consciousness. The *bhaktic* element injected into Hinduism a strong dose of the "love of God"; and among the Australian aborigines, totemic celebrations, which imply a common life shared by man and nature, are accompanied, as Elkin has shown, by a mythology that indicates that this life is a personal or quasi personal one.[18] These are no doubt valid but certainly not apodictic considerations. Therefore we would probably encounter fewer difficulties from Buddhist and Hindu

17. *Hinduism*, p. 92.
18. *The Australian Aborigines*, p. 223.

groups were we to differentiate the "religious mind" from the secular mentality as one in which truth is primarily action, that is, as one in which the thrust toward knowledge is secondary to the "deliverance" motif. Then, of course, we must redefine "personal" to align it with this new perspective.

Eliade has exploited the Buddhist passages which speak of breaking through a roof or flying through the air, figures which in context betoken a passage from the conditioned to the unconditioned mode of existence *(Nirvāna, Asamskṛta, Samādhi,* etc.)[19] Arhats shatter roofs and ascend into the sky—a figurative way of expressing their transcendence of the human condition. These images, constants of Indian thought, are intended to suggest the irruption of the ordinary situation of life, a breakthrough of those natural cosmic arrangements which have formed one of the dialectical poles of religious thought from archaic times until our own and are, for that very reason, a built-in temptation to worldliness and spiritual corruption. The religious sense of these images is their opening us to the "beyond," to a world uncontaminated by human expediency, pro-tem values, and feckless change. Unlike the profane world of natural science, this sacred world, called into existence by the insight that distinguishes contingent from absolute, does not esteem the principle of knowledge for knowledge's sake. It has been revealed to us in order to illuminate the dimension of liberation and thus to elicit our initiative and cooperation in the arduous task of overcoming finitude. The yogic techniques, for instance, can be interpreted as stages in the progressive cosmic integration of man: efforts to transform the chaos of biomental life into the rhythmic life of a cosmos.

For the Western man the difficulty of incorporating these spiritual views into a religious framework is their un-

19. See, for example, "Structures and Changes in the History of Religion," pp. 365–66.

abashed antipersonalism. "But, for India," Eliade has re-marked,

> what matters most is not so much the salvation of the *personality* as obtaining *absolute freedom*. (We shall see later that the deep meaning of this freedom leaves the most extreme Western formulations far behind; what the Indian actually wants is, in a certain sense, to abolish creation by reincorporating all forms in the primordial Unity.) Once it is granted that this freedom cannot be gained in our present human condition and that personality is the vehicle of suffering and drama, it becomes clear that what must be sacrificed is the human condition and the "personality."[20]

This use of quotation marks on "personality" should alert us to our need for *re-* (or refined) definition. If "person" or "personality" refers simply to the individual (in our loose, Western usage we talk this way; our inheritance of Roman law and Protestant theology inclines us to equate personal rights with the individual), then the Indian insistence upon the primordial unity or Undivided as the fulfillment and true meaning of the individual becomes incomprehensible. But if we think these terms in the light of Hegel's Master–Slave dialectic—its point, we recall, is the struggle for personal recognition—or from the angle of Buber's I–Thou relationship, then, as Emil Brunner has suggested, we might more readily look upon being a person as an act, not as a condition or state of nature. The image of an individual as a private enclosed garden is a perversion, for personality is a wholeness achieved through an openness to "the other."

Although the consequences of this viewpoint have circulated everywhere, it should be helpful to note some of them explicitly. First, the "human person" should be thought dynamically, not statically. Rather than a once-and-for-all given, the person is someone who develops or is retarded

20. *Yoga: Immortality and Freedom*, p. 35.

through contact with other persons, and therefore the rule-of-thumb gauge of "personality" has to be the ability to relate personally to others. Because someone can be physically present to another without entering into a maturing personal relationship with him, it is clear that one's personality refers to something that transcends, and cannot be explained by, purely biological and physical nature. Second, this transcendence of mere physical presence through the gift of self can be generally classified as an attitude toward the world. But like all human attitudes, it is essentially precarious; it is constantly menaced by temptations to retraction, self-preoccupation, and isolation. (In Buddhist terms, this flight from "personality" is the work of the self, the source of that deeply rooted selfishness which inevitably causes suffering.) Yet as a form of activity, "the personal" likewise tends to permeate all of one's activities. Through fostering a respect for the dignity of ("the divine" in) others, it compels one to live in accord with the deeper meaning of the Master–Slave dialectic: "I am not a thing or just another object." Exercised within a religious context, it brings the believer to the final goal of a personal experience of God. It spills over, as the Buddhists have always stressed, into one's dealings with all living creatures, but even beyond that into inanimate nature, which likewise can be treated with respect or cruelly misused. Third, the dynamism of "personality" is antagonistic to rugged individualism. By stressing the function of the group or "the other" in personal development and enrichment, it points to the paradox of man's essential finitude: liberation requires communion. In this way the philosophical notion of a negation at the very core of man's being is related theologically to the Gospel paradox of having to lose one's life in order to find it.

It should be evident how these remarks on "personality" are relevant to our initial question of distinguishing the religious from the secular mind, specifically, to answering the query: Is the world ultimately personal or impersonal?

Natural science, although a relating or unifying activity that discloses the natural thrust of human understanding toward a total vision of things, is silent on this question, and for various reasons, naturalists rule out any attempt to break this primordial silence. In the main, they are likely to consider the speculations of cosmologists as adequate or at best as sufficient for our present circumstances; they tend to be unimpressed by the religionists' data; they are convinced that a rewarding and meaningful existence can be led without recourse to "primitive fancies" or religious hypotheses. Ultimately, the world is not personal, but man achieves himself and a better world by trying to make a cosmos out of chaos.

In contrast, the religious mind is wedded to a pronounced personalist view of things, either in the form of creator gods or other deities who control the world and man's destiny, or in the shape of an acosmological and transpersonal sort of ascesis that aims at a deliverance of the true self (the "person"), whether through union with Brahman-God or with Brahman-self. Zaehner has clarified this last point in his description of the classic monist ontology of the ninth-century Śankara, who

admits of no distinction at all between the liberated soul and the Absolute or the liberated soul and God *quâ* Absolute. He does not deny the existence of the Creator God on the empirical level nor does he identify the soul with this God on any level. Creation, omnipotence, and omniscience are the attributes of God as seen by man while still in the bondage of *māyā* ["illusion, ignorance"]: let us call these attributes *māyā (a)*. Dependence, limited knowledge, and limited power are among the attributes of the man not yet liberated: let us call them *māyā (b)*. God, then, will be Brahman + *māyā (a)*, man Brahman + *māyā (b)*. But from the absolute point of view *māyā* does not exist; so

man and God must be identically Brahman. On the
relative level, however, they are distinct since their
māyās are different. The identity, however, is the
reality, and this is what *moksha* reveals.[21]

In the preceding chapters we have constantly reverted to
this distinction of absolute and relative, of how things really
are from how they appear to us, because of the singular role
that it has played in Western philosophy since the time of
Descartes. But we were unable to confine our discussions
to epistemology. Ineluctably we found ourselves sweeping
wider horizons since questions touching the nature of
knowledge extend out to—and are themselves determined
by—views about man, his world, the Real, and therefore
God. Here, then, in a classic form of Indian thought we find
a confirmation of these earlier reflections. If Eastern
thinkers have also detected a schism at the core of man's
world and knowledge, can we not rightfully suppose that
we are dealing with a universal human experience, and so
with the fundamental structures of man's consciousness in
discerning and coping with it? For this reason this Eastern,
emphatically non-Kantian, resolution is particularly in-
structive. It is, first of all, a religious solution, one that binds
up the schism within man himself and thus heals the breach
between man and his world. In other words, like the Western apologetic of knowledge, it focuses on religious thought
as holistic, as a total view that allows us to discriminate between the absolute and the contingent. *Moksha,* besides, is
a delivering or salvific knowledge; it entails conversion or
rebirth. Thus the incisive moment of religious experience is
a revelation, for through regeneration or through becoming
a new creature the ordinary or natural way of looking at
the world is ruptured, and the sense of the normal shines
through. In Christianity and several other religions, a person "speaks," and in his word the meaning of nature and

history—of man's personal world—is unfolded. Nature and history, therefore, are not apologetically neutral or binding authorities. They are, on the contrary, the deposits of shared experience: the narratives, we might say, that keep experiences available for comparison. Reflective Easterners continue to detect a schism within Western man, whose religions obviously have not healed him. Now that all parts of the globe are being swamped by Western technology, non-Westerners view with alarm the very "despiritualizing influence of our current science industry" that Nietzsche heralded. They espy us in anxious search for a substitute, having lost God in the eighteenth and nineteenth centuries and having lost Man in the twentieth. Malraux has transcribed their vision into words:

Your moderate attempts to construct a moderate nihilism do not seem destined to long life . . . What awareness can you have of this universe, on which you have based your unanimity, and which you call reality? . . . The history of the psychological life of Europeans, of the new Europe, is a record of the invasion of the mind by emotions which are made chaotic by their conflicting intensities. The image of all these men dedicated to maintaining an idea of Man which allows them to overcome their thought and live, while the world over which this Man reigns becomes each day more foreign to them, is doubtless the final vision I shall take away from the West.[22]

But have our Eastern-oriented critics gone to the heart of the matter in order to study these dichotomies of our thought? Do they recognize that the antireligious thrust of our philosophy stems from an analytically scientific cast of mind that is contemptuous of the synthetically metaphysical? Until recently our philosophers spoke often of

22. *The Temptation of the West,* Eng. trans. Robert Hollander (New York, Random House, 1961), pp. 97–98.

nature, almost never of person: the generic took precedence over the specific, the species over the individual, the abstract over the concrete. They cultivated exclusively, in Lévi-Strauss' figure, the sharpened edge of "the most fundamental form of knowledge, and the only one that we all have in common," and so sacrificed substance for the keenness of scientific penetration. Regrettably, this procedure is efficacious provided only that we can penetrate "far enough so that the whole bulk of the instrument follow the sharpened point."[23]

From the rapid survey presented in this chapter we have perhaps gleaned—or at least recognized from the thrust of Eliade's thought—the truth of Edward Tylor's remark: that no religion of mankind lies in utter isolation from the rest. Thus the thoughts and principles of Christianity are attached to intellectual clues that run back through pre-Christian ages to the very origin of human civilization. Although we may have sacrificed some sharpness of focus for our phenomenology by not further pursuing these clues, still we have gone far enough to discern in the general patterns of religious thought a unifying consciousness that construes the man–world–God ensemble in holistic, personal terms. Literally, this universe takes on comprehensive features, a *persona* or character that permits one to find his way about. Western science, on the contrary, owes its success to an "objectifying" abstraction that depersonalizes man and desacramentalizes his universe. The clues to life's meaning and self-revelation have become scrambled in formalizations and limited concerns. Interested outsiders read the Western literature of anxiety that is symptomatic of a resultant spiritual malaise, in wonder, to be sure, why we have found no suggested remedy for our meaninglessness. Can we not learn a lesson from our extensive anthropological investigation of the Bororo?

23. Claude Lévi-Strauss, *Tristes Tropiques*, Eng. trans. John Russell (New York, Atheneum, 1964), p. 127.

These Brazilian primitives, Lévi-Strauss informs us, became completely disoriented when the Salesian missionaries forced them out of the regularity of their village life as an expedient for converting them.

> All feeling for their traditions would desert them, as if their social and religious systems (these were inseparable, as we shall see) were so complex that they could not exist without the schema made visible in their ground-plans and reaffirmed to them in the daily rhythm of their lives.[24]

Is it not also true for us that personal signs are wiped out by the exacting regularity and strict causal determinations of science? Naturally the world of science has nothing to say about freedom and love, the staples from time immemorial of life and religious commitment.

It is an anomaly of these two outlooks on the world, the scientific and the religious, that the former is compulsive and the latter is free. The history of apologetics notwithstanding, it is essential to any act of faith that it be a free response, which means nothing less than that there is no unique or intellectually coercive set of motives for this choice, although reasons for such an option are readily contrived. In this sense also reflective religion will always be personal and existential, and therefore will share in a type of thought that is still popularly called existentialism. Since no philosopher of our times has matched the fervor of these existentialists in exploring the theistic–atheistic commitment, their thought invites us to an intriguing perusal. The better-know Sartrean view, summed up in the eloquence of *No Exit,* will challenge us in the following chapter, for it has posed the problem of personalism in all of its concrete urgency: "Hell is other people."

24. Ibid., p. 204.

EIGHT. THE FATE OF COMMITMENT

> The individual, abandoned, lost in an indifferent or hostile society, coils about himself and attempts to find recourse in immanence against impossible transcendence.
>
> SARTRE, *Saint Genet*

There is a danger that an invitation to review Sartre's production will be rejected out of hand as *déjà vu*. He has suffered popularity. Many of the causes he championed have slipped into historical memory, and with them the literature and propaganda that they occasioned. The palinodal quality of *The Words* is unmistakable, yet we are uncertain about which of his works to exempt from this apparently wholesale condemnation. Even the existentialism riveted to his name has disappeared into the philosophic limbo. The postwar vapor of despair that had been charged by the struggles of the thirties, by the national humiliation of 1940, by the German occupation, the underground, and the agonies of deportation has lifted, giving us a different view from the Café de Flore and Les Deux Magots. Nevertheless, however we may judge his literary output and philosophical talent, we cannot ignore the deep inner tensions and ambiguous ethical situations of Sartrean man. Avowedly this is a moralist's artistic creation, but one who steadfastly holds the mirror to the twentieth-century visage. He makes us look with unflinching eye at brutal consequences. "I killed God," the character Goetz confided in *The Devil and the Good Lord,* "because he divided me from mankind, and now I see that his death has isolated me even more surely. I shall not allow this huge carcass to poison my human friend-ships; I shall tell the whole truth, if necessary."[1]

Sartre has told us much of the truth in *The Words*. Before that self-disclosure, however, we were probably inclined to take his *Existentialism is a Humanism* at face value, without attributing psychological motives to its frank confessions. His atheism was simply an intellectual conviction that rested on the foundations of traditional French radicalism: that nothing will be changed if God does not exist; that we shall rediscover the same norms of honesty, progress, and humanity when we have disposed of God as an out-of-date hypothesis destined to die quietly of itself. There was nothing new in the proposal. "Religious" humanists had for a long time maintained that the goal of man's life is the complete realization of his personality in the here and now, because "the nature of the universe depicted by modern science makes unacceptable any super-natural or cosmic guarantees of human values."[2] But since *The Words* we read the humanism essay with our gaze fixed on freedom and over against the smug, phony world of the child who believed in progress because, no doubt, his grandfather, Charles Schweitzer, did. Progress, however, for that child meant the long, steep path leading to himself. His environment, he tells us, made him into an actor and a willing victim of proverbial bad faith. Indeed, the irony with which he speaks in *The Words* of the related problems of contingency, absurdity, and ontological necessity suggests that it is the fate of isolated children who have been surrounded by attitudinizing adults who delight in "putting necessity everywhere" to become obsessed by the problem of justifying their own existence.

1. Eng. trans. Kitty Black (New York, Random House, Vintage edition, 1962), p. 147.

2. *A Humanist Manifesto*, first published in *The New Humanist* (First Series), *6* (1933), reproduced as a monograph by The American Humanist Association, 1952.

Sartre's autobiographical work at the time of this writing is still incomplete. His genius, brilliantly described as discovering one's way out of desperate circumstances, has displayed itself not merely in finding normalcy through books and writing but also—undoubtedly the reaction of anyone who stares for a long time at the "banality of evil" —in ripping the veneer off progress and in debasing the myth of a world of modern science which does not answer to man's basic needs and choices. The profound philosophical issues Sartre has raised reach the inmost heart and spirit of man, the "useless passion." Our freedom, he has argued, is more than an immediate call for a moral decision. It is, fundamentally, an ontological issue, for upon it rests our world, with or without God. The contemporary theologian therefore misses the point if he supposes that all he has to contend with are the rationalizations, the window-dressing of modern science. For behind the montage stands a more radical humanism. "Contemporary disbelief," Camus once remarked, "no longer relies on science as it did at the end of the last century. It denies both science and religion. It is no longer a skeptical reaction to miracles. It is passionate disbelief."[3] Passionate, perhaps, but not nihilistic. For Camus and others who have shared his sentiment of "keeping faith with the earth," of building here a genuine city of peace that represents more than a tragic hope, all confess an extraordinary faith in man.

I continue to believe that this world has no supernatural meaning. But I know that something in the world has meaning—man—because he is the only being who demands meaning for himself. This world at least contains the truth of man, and our task is to justify him in the face of destiny itself.[4]

3. A contribution to *La Vie intellectuelle* (1949), 349, cited by John Cruickshank, *Albert Camus and the Literature of Revolt* (New York, Oxford University Press, 1960).
4. Camus, *Lettres à un ami allemand* (Paris, Gallimard, 1945), pp. 72–73.

In the last chapter we saw that the hinge of Eliade's thought is the dialectic of the Sacred. Just as Kant recognized that man's phenomenal knowledge is limited by, and projected in terms of, an ideal, noumenal reasoning, so in similar fashion Eliade has explicated the Sacred and the Profane, the transcendent plane of absolute values, in dynamic interplay with the immediate area of contingent experience. The subtlety of this dialectic should not blind us to its claim: that it is the encounter with the Sacred which permits us to discourse about the Profane; in fact, that it is the experience of the Sacred that generates such ideas as *reality, truth,* and *meaning.* Were it not for this irruption which stimulates us to ask what is real or true, there would be no philosophical or scientific knowledge at all.

Although dialectic has had many meanings in the history of philosophy, even among the Greeks who coined the term, in contemporary thought one instinctively conjures up the image of Hegel when he hears it, even though he may be referring to Sartre or Eliade. For this reason it is important that we understand the Hegelian usage. Thought, for Hegel, is dialectic: the process or movement of *Aufhebung.* In this, of course, he was opposing the Kantian scientific or categorical conception, not merely because Kant took over his categories uncriticized and thereby exposed himself to charges of superficiality and inadequacy, but also because of the theological impasse into which he inevitably led us. The Kantian position is precisely that the Absolute is unknowable. One must think the Unconditioned if he is to think at all. But how can an ontological Unconditioned be justified from empiricist premises; how can it avoid strangling us in the net of Spinoza's pantheism? The dichotomy of Kant is complete: knowledge versus faith, time versus eternity, thought versus being, man versus God. In a word, the alienation of master from slave has been set.

To all appearances Sartre has appropriated the Marxian

critique of alienation, and Eliade's research has corrobo-
rated the feeling that religious thought perishes without a
reconciling image. Similarities notwithstanding, we must
emphasize the differences between Eliade and Sartre. Since
both are dialectical, they witness conspicuously to the contradictory purposes to which thought can be put. Thought,
accordingly, is an instrument but not just a tool of unbridled
passion. Both of these thinkers, certainly, have thought passionately; but, following Hegel, they appeal to a norm of
truth beyond mere opinion and immediate self-certitude.
Each offers us, in reality, a form of experience called "reason" and asks us to justify our reasonings by testing the
consistency of this experience.

Eliade, as we have seen, accepts the fact we express as
best we can in the vague phrase: "Experience engenders
thought." (Ordinarily we try to diminish the time interval
of this activity by indicating that thought itself is an experience, but this usage frequently confuses matters.) "Experiencing" we might picture to ourselves as the act in or by
which we are shaken out of the routine or spontaneous. An
occurrence stimulates our reflective process (thought, dialectic) so that we distinguish and talk about experiencing
and call certain facets of it "spontaneous" or "routine."
Eliade's interest is religious experience: an irruption of the
Sacred, a revelation, a manifestation of the holy that stirs our
reflection so that we "experience"—actually, distinguish on
reflection—the extraordinary or different, and therefore we
designate its counterpart "profane." From this description
of the thought process, two important points emerge. First,
reflection never begins absolutely. It commences from, and
is upon, an experience which is appealed to as a norm or
guideline throughout the dialectical movement. Thus the
once philosophically respectable image of the "mind" as a
tabula rasa is dangerously misleading. Second, the dialectical nature of thought and experience—and all of their
surrogates: meaning, truth, etc.—brings into prominence

the aspect of human understanding that Kant highlighted: dependence, or otherness. For penetrating the Sartrean man, this notion is indispensable.

When we read *The Words,* we are apt to confirm an impression that Sartre's atheism is concretely, like all other atheisms, a revolt against a milieu and the particular religious forms it treasured. For Sartre it is evident that God never really lived. Conventional church attendance was a part of bourgeois respectability; so that when these fake values were swept away in the struggle for authenticity, mere words—theological doctrines, pious cant, and the like—were naturally discarded. Yet it is clear that what troubled Sartre was the otherness of God. He has reserved his choicest venom for the doctrine of Creation because, for the Judaeo-Christian world in which he has lived, it keynotes man's essential dependence; figuratively, his standing with his hat out to receive both his freedom and the bounty of grace so that he might be finally adjudged worthy or unworthy of his predestination by an all-knowing and all-powerful Master. Sartre's imagination could not, and cannot, tolerate such a degrading pose.

But there is more to Sartre's position than that. Despite their other disagreements, Maurice Merleau-Ponty, who praised philosophy's independence of theism and atheism alike by ridiculing efforts to cut off further questions either by an "apocalypse of Wonderland" or a "mystique of the superman," would have us believe—and in this he was undoubtedly an authentic Sartrean—that metaphysics and morals perish in contact with an absolute.[5] When we return to Sartre, the suggestion becomes clearer that not just the once-and-for-all absolute but any form of otherness is a threat to our freedom because it implies that we must submit to, conform to, or in some other way be limited by, the extraneous and uncontrollable. God is only the extreme case of what is a fantastically hellish situation. "The con-

5. *Sens et Non-sens,* pp. 190–91.

sciousness of others," Sartre noted in the book on Genet, "is the medium in which man can and must become what he is."[6] And yet these other consciousnesses "bring us to light" (expose us), "know" us as Adam "knew" his wife (dominated her), and treat us as objects. Their gaze catches us, so that there is no exit from this shame and subtle death.

It is not sufficient to dismiss Sartre's keyhole situation, with its passing references to Kafka's *The Trial* and *The Castle,* as the creation of a misanthrope, although the idea that others steal our being or rape us by looking at us or make us guilty borders on the perverted. Yet Sartre, it would appear, has simply taken over the Hegelian analysis of life with others, which Hegel said was founded on desire *(Begierde).* Our consumption of objects of knowledge was analogous, he surmised, to our hunger for food (in both cases our incompleteness prompts a quest, a perpetual towardness in our being), and the high price of self-consciousness depicted in the Master–Slave dialectic (that is, domination and the devouring of another's freedom) is a matter of historical record: that each consciousness pursues the death of the other. Hegel's dialectic of the Jena period was centered on life, that of the *Phenomenology* on freedom. In both he was talking about the death of spirit and intelligence through stultification and resistance to change. His message of growth through contradiction and opposition strikes us as only less individualized than Sartre's, more intellectually detached than the moralist's concrete presentation of the choices mirrored in masochism, sadism, hatred, indifference, and love. The Hegelian conflict of consciousnesses and Sartre's notion of the emergence of another consciousness effecting an internal hemorrhage of my world *(No Exit)* has also been dramatized by Simone de Beauvoir in *L'Invitée (She Came to Stay)* and *The Mandarins.*

6. *Saint Genet, Actor and Martyr,* Eng. trans. Bernard Frechtman (New York, Braziller), 1963, p. 549.

This use of the theater to explore the various possibilities of man—the metaphysical myths of his situation in the world, his psychological capacities, the social aspects of his actual problems—has also been identified with the names of Marcel, Anouilh, Montherlant, and Camus. It has the obvious advantage of offering us a slice of life with its conflicts heightened for our moral evaluation. In the past critical decisions touching collaboration, the war, the underground, and so on were limned. Today we have other threats to our freedom and creativity: the encroachments of the machine and business organization, a demand to surrender to the conformities of the Great Society, and countless other personal conflicts ranging from interior debates over the justice of war through racial and ethnic equality and justice to personal religious responsibility clashing with obsolete rules and traditions. But Sartre, as we know now, never intended just a topical social commentary. All of these are perennially significant choices, but they are lost opportunities if they fail to illuminate our basically absurd situation. Ontic freedom, in Heidegger's vocabulary, has its interest, but our preoccupation with it must not prevent us from weighing the paradoxes of our ontological freedom. Philosophically Sartre would have us take a step beyond the inexplicable woven into every human life that we confess in everyday jargon: *C'est la vie*—That's the way the ball bounces. He would have us enter into Malraux's "metallic kingdom of absurdity" to meditate the absurdity of the Absurd: a need for transcendence (the fact that we must choose in order to be and to complete ourselves) that gives wings to an intoxicating freedom which cannot rationalize itself and therefore leaves us with frustrating, haunting "why's." All of us, no doubt, are aware of the fate of Orestes when we read:

Suddenly, out of the blue, freedom crashed down on me and swept me off my feet. Nature sprang back, my youth

164   *Reflective Theology*

went with the wind, and I knew myself alone, utterly alone in the midst of this well-meaning little universe of yours. I was like a man who's lost his shadow. And there was nothing left in heaven, no right or wrong, nor anyone to give me orders.[7]

We have said that Sartre is profoundly Hegel oriented, and that his dialectical reflection upon man's contingency has been inspired by Spinoza's celebrated dictum: determination is negation. Since knowledge consists in determining (distinguishing, defining), it follows that human consciousness of its essence negates and is, therefore, in Sartre's language ultimately a nothing, a *néant*. Hence man is not first conscious and then free, but his very act of determining consciousness constitutes his fundamental act of choice. Because man is "not enough," he wants to be. Primarily, then, he chooses to be aware, to open himself to "the other," and this is a fatal option since it is the choice that puts him in the predicament of endless conflict and self-destroying tension. "To be" in the complete or full sense would mean that man "has arrived," that he no longer has need of "the other" in order to attain himself. But this is tantamount to the end of freedom, to a stagnant existence in which, as for Hegel, all the cows would be black. In a nutshell, Sartre has seen all of our woes as stemming from negation. The continuously recurring themes of his exposition—situation, facticity, contingency, finitude—revert to this fundamental act, the portentous decision to be an individual. In this he reminds us of the Buddhist, but one who denies us, as we shall see, any transcendence to Buddhahood.

The contrast of this dialectic with that of Eliade is remarkable. According to Eliade's perspective reflection begins from or in an inaugurating experience, an irruption

7. *The Flies*, Act III, Eng. trans. Stuart Gilbert (New York, Random House, Vintage book), pp. 121–22.

of the Sacred which for the sake of comparison can be likened to the irruption of consciousness. Because thought or dialectic is an articulation and testing of this experience, an indissoluble link is forged between the two. Consequently, to the degree that man grasps this link and submits himself to the discipline of wrestling with its components, he achieves himself as a person. Sartre, on the other hand, has preferred to picture thought as creating experience. His esteem for freedom has led him to equate the choice to be aware with the choice of a "world." We struggle to make a life worth living, and in so doing create ourselves and the values that we cherish. A complementary perspective, we might say; but a consideration of its consequences can only convince us that this was a hasty and immature judgment.

In *The Words* Sartre more closely approximates Eliade. He has spoken of his childhood experience as an inaugurating experience, one that formed the negative pole of play-acting and bad faith against which he subsequently reacted. As a result, perhaps, of this traumatic experience Sartre has designedly emphasized the negative aspect of dialectic; it is not an articulation but a repulsion of experience. Experience destroys unless we negate it, whereas in Eliade's view experience is a wellspring of enrichment. For Sartre man is a useless passion because by freely choosing to be conscious he has constituted himself as a desire for Being, ultimately for God. He has, willy-nilly, condemned himself to knowledge, which is a "deflowering," a "violation." He suffers the passion of having to transcend himself, of being coerced to open himself (if he wants to be human) to the degrading and overwhelming Other. This, indeed, is to suggest that Sartrean man is not merely Hegelian man who becomes through negation, but that he is ("Man *is* freedom") by that negation which is a flight from otherness. Sartre was not exaggerating when he wrote in the first number of *Les Temps modernes:* "We are with those who want to change both man's social condition and the conception which he has of himself." For he is only *l'homme révolté;* not one who thrives by interpersonal relations but who exists only by denying both God and other people. To find himself he had to lose others.

> As a result, my pure choice did not raise me above anyone. Without equipment, without tools, I set all of me to work in order to save all of me. If I relegate impossible Salvation to the proproom, what remains? A whole man, composed of all men and as good as all of them and no better than any.[8]

Sartre's choice is a pure one: unmotivated, uncaused, existential. He escapes the dilemma over causal determination and inexplicable freedom that has plagued modern philosophers since Spinoza by locating choice in a Kierkegaardian existential category. Yet even though this is the leap that begins life's course and is, therefore, unjustifiable a priori ("absurd"), it is still a moral act. (Sartre at this point is curiously reminiscent of Saint Thomas.) We are henceforth "without excuse": responsible for all the consequences of this fatal move. In the concrete, especially with Sartre himself and Genet in mind, it is not difficult to grasp this point. We are familiar with the idea of self-appropriation; ingrained attitudes and conventional viewpoints must be challenged in the light of novel and personal situations. For this reason Sartre is more convincing in his autobiography and in the Genet book; less so, perhaps, when treating Baudelaire or Flaubert. We can sympathize with a pursuit of freedom and integrity through negation and rebellion. But why must we be so adamant about this primordial choice to be conscious? Is it such a total choice of self that it pervades absolutely everything? Even the formal characteristics of Genet's style, Sartre believes, his composition, the

8. *The Words*, Eng. trans. Bernard Frechtman (New York, Braziller, 1964), p. 255.

structure of his imagery, his particular tastes "retrace in detail the story of a liberation."[9]

When reading Sartre, one may wonder which came first, the concern for freedom or the theory of consciousness. Whatever the answer may be, it is evident that they fit together hand in glove. For if consciousness is a negation, a denial of otherness that sets one's teeth on edge and colors his entire attitude toward the transcendent, then evidently he must rally his immanent forces in order to pit them against the opposition. One "takes charge" or "conducts" himself by taking the necessary means (does what he thinks right or good) to create or defend his integrity. If consciousness is freedom, albeit of this defensive sort, and creative of its values, then it it not only responsible but totally responsible. In this way the thesis of absolute freedom requires total responsibility, which in turn demands a pellucid consciousness. Sartre has rejected Freud's explanatory Unconscious.

For our purpose, nothing is to be gained by subjecting the basic assumption of *Being and Nothingness,* Sartre's *en-soi/pour-soi* dichotomy, to a rigorous critique. This has been amply done by professional philosophers. But what ought to be contributory to our estimate of his position is a radical defect of this work which seems traceable to his leitmotif of choice. For Sartre apparently assumed that it was a sufficient justification of his starting-point to assert that because consciousness is always *of* something (pure towardness or intentionality), it must be defined as a negation. It simply *is not,* in the case, that is, that the scope of the factual is material reality. At this point Sartre seems dangerously close to that sensism which at one time Camus professed. At any rate, the presumption of his reader is that this point of view will be argued in his book, formally by preference, but otherwise through confirmatory examples. But as things develop, the plausible becomes definitive in

9. *Saint Genet,* French edition of Gallimard (1952), p. 536.

terms of this postulated ontology. When we look for a justification of the basic stance, we are referred back to it as a maxim: "This is because . . . " "Everything happens as if . . . " Our intention, of course, is not to belabor the obvious unsatisfactoriness of this method, but to emphasize its grounding in Sartre's vision of things. There is only intuitive knowledge, he maintained: another way of stating that knowledge is an absolute and primitive event. Either we see things his way or we don't. What is quintessential is that we take all the consequences of our chosen prospect.

Although Sartre has advocated freedom on the grounds that there is no passage from "is" to "ought" (ontology, in other words, cannot support an ethic), it is evident to his reader and Simone de Beauvoir's that the philosophy presented is in reality an ethic, that is, the advocacy of a course of action built upon a lived ontology. In *La Force des choses* for instance, Beauvoir has described the failure of the French Left to carry through the revolution that seemed promised by the triumph of the resistance movement in 1944, as well as its chagrin, not to say humiliation, at seeing its own solution for the Algerian problem successfully applied by a paternalistic and aging general. In addition she has conveyed a mood of profound pessimism, stemming from the gnawing failure to feel a sense of personal recognition after having fulfilled her ambitions. Thus her first volume of autobiography, the *Mémoires d'une jeune fille rangée,* which began as a quickening story of self-discovery and self-liberation, has deteriorated into an irreligious Book of Job, a curmudgeonly complaint about the vanity of vanities. Her most recent contribution to the literature of despair, occasioned by the painful death of her mother, is unlikely to gain her a following among the enthusiastic young. This pensive existentialism no longer has a venturesome appeal; it betrays, rather, the regrets of a disenchanted intellectual prig. For the old clarion calls seem hollow now, or tame: that the absurdity of existence cannot be justified by the traditional values, God, Humanity; that men must learn to live authentically in an indifferent, even hostile, world; that we must take the fullest responsibility for the values we create; that no one, when he looks at Genet and others who have been sacrificed to social expediency, can accept society and its preachments without challenge; that life, finally, is relentless conflict, interior and exterior. We have our own peculiar problems to solve without clinging nostalgically to those of the postwar years. And since Sartre, above all, has taught us that his philosophical superstructure is merely a justification of his commitment—has he not stated in *La Critique de la raison dialectique* that Marxism is the only true philosophy; existentialism is an ideology?—we are less inclined to be moved by the inner logic of declared partisan arguments.

This Sartrean superstructure carries a strongly Spinozistic undertone for the trained philosopher. From the *en-soi*, the totality, emanates the "being" of consciousness, which resists a natural pull toward reabsorption by trying to establish itself as another en-soi. We are tempted to project this struggle against a Taoist or Buddhist (Nirvāna) horizon, but Sartre was too much the moralist, too concerned about freedom, to think in these patterns. Yet he could not totally avoid them. As a "negative" emanation, the *pour-soi* "is," that is to say "has meaning," only in terms of the en-soi; its futility consists in its having to assert itself continuously in opposition to its dialectical counterpart. Man is the being pledged to solitude, not to communion.

This image appears even more strikingly in contrasting Sartre's analysis of death with Heidegger's. The import of Heidegger's clarifications of *Sein und Zeit* is that all along he was interested in Being, the totality, the *Grund,* so that death in his thought is to be contemplated as a sign of man's finitude. From a standpoint in Being, man thinks his limitation and freely accepts it. The poise is typically Heideggerian: one thinks the finite from the Ground while bracketing the infinite. It is, indeed, the charisma of the aerialist to start from the Whole without thinking the Whole. Sartre, on the contrary, has chosen freedom: he thinks the part, the individual, as over against the Whole, and the part's passion to become itself a whole. Death, therefore, marks a solemn end for this free individual, since meaning has been introduced into the world by the individual's consciousness. It is a lonely but heroic stand.

> Yet, in the depth of their solitude, it was the others that they were protecting, all the others, all their comrades in the Resistance. Total responsibility in total solitude—is not this the very definition of our liberty? This being stripped of all, this solitude, this tremendous danger, were the same for all . . . Each of them, standing against the oppressors, undertook to be himself, freely and irrevocably. And by choosing for himself in freedom, he chose the freedom of all.[10]

The nobility of this stance does not palliate the harsh truth of Sartrean man: condemned to freedom he is a frustrated god, *un Dieu manqué.* In his offering of a way out of desperate circumstances, Sartre has not always impressed us with the personal cast of his thought. The stress on negation as a withdrawal was always a feature of his writings, but the idea that this was the refusal of a childhood world never quite came through to us in the insistence upon the choice of consciousness itself as the constitution of a world. In other words, this commitment to consciousness, Sartre's peculiar choice of a world, was presented as an ontology. But as soon as we correct this false perspective on a universal claim, then the possibility of another view, as plausible, trenchant, consistent, and maybe as congenial as Sartre's, suggests itself. If Sartre's

10. *The Republic of Silence,* Eng. trans. Ramon Guthrie, compiled and edited by A. J. Liebling (New York, Harcourt, Brace & World, 1947), pp. 498–500.

negation has focused alienation, refusal, and inevitable opposition, is it not equally valuable to restore the balance by Gabriel Marcel's option? Instead of a seedbed of hostility, negation can be cultivated as the matrix of love. Human longing may be less a desire to be God than an instinct to commune, for the paradox of love is that true union demands an unalterable otherness. In this option, the agony of division is not the whole story; it is compensated for by an ecstasy of fulfillment.

The projection of the contingencies of one's personal life—in this instance of Sartre's smothering experience of the otherness of consciousness—into a paradigm case is excusable but procedurally questionable. But aside from this objection to his presentation, the fact that he had to find himself through a rejection of an imposed value system may account for a way of talking about freedom, self-appropriation, or creativity that is unfaithful to his actual starting-point. For one can trumpet the blessings of freedom and creativity in such a manner that we forget how the choice to be aware is hopelessly tangled in the intentionality of consciousness. Sartre's own stark realism should correct some of our misconceptions. But in all this heady talk about freedom, we need firm reminders that consciousness is always *of* something, that it is a mode of apprehending (experience, reality, the Transcendent: whatever may indicate that complex which we know in our experiencing), in which a selective or creative aspect functions in coordination with, and under the guidance or control of, the reality we express. By beginning from the en-soi, Sartre actually affirmed that his dialectic, like Eliade's, took wings from experience. It commenced with the rupture of consciousness (pour-soi): an intuition, an insight, a revelation that was creative because it affected one's whole outlook and was a mode of apprehension that was simultaneously individual (in that sense a free choice) and compulsory (indicative of how things really are). Sartre was right: there is a dictatorship about the Other; we do not create knowledge in a vacuum. The ultimate paradox of the situation is that we have to be faithful ("We *must* choose") to an insight that we know is not divine, not the absolute truth, not utterly exhaustive. Sartre's childhood taught him, long before he read Nietzsche, that truth is a value. His intention, presumably, in meditating on the ethics of knowledge was to make us painfully aware of the abtractive nature of the thought (and its articulation in the further abstraction of language) to which we must freely commit ourselves. How much more "absurd" can we get?

To end his analysis of commitment on a note of absurdity may have been a miscalculation on Sartre's part. Because this word readily suggests the notion of blind choice, many theologians have been reluctant to address themselves to his position either as a serious intellectual construction or as a lived reality. They sense, rightfully, that a policy of "Declare your intuitions, no matter what the rest of the world may say," or of offering one's own experience as a blueprint for the world, is eventually self-defeating. The fact that these descriptions have enjoyed a literary vogue is immaterial; they will be carried away by the next wind of fashion.

To adopt this attitude is singularly myopic. It is unfortunate that one can readily magnify the inadequacies of Sartre's presentation since he has created the impression that dire consequences follow inexorably from the primal choice of consciousness, as if his own life were not a testimonial in behalf of change or growth. Yet we cannot allow ourselves to be absorbed by the peripheral. Certainly in a more concrete way than any of his direct philosophical ancestors—if not more clearly—Sartre has pondered what it means to say that dialectic is a scheme of unifying or relating. Are we aware, he asks, of our principles of order? Like Kant, have we merely assumed that our categories are the proper ones, the only ones? Do we understand to what we have committed ourselves by choosing a certain pattern?

We scarcely need to be reminded that the dialectical label applies in quite different ways to the thought of Fichte, Hegel, Marx, and Kierkegaard, not to mention Proudhon. Sartre's novelty, if his reputation is to hang upon this commodity, is not that he asked this question, but the peculiar light or dimension into which he projected it. Central to any dialectic is the idea of otherness. It was Sartre's destiny to proclaim in the ontology of *Being and Nothingness* that this otherness is fundamentally inimical to man.

Philosophers from the time of Descartes have been meditating the problem of knowledge. It was Descartes' genius to have called upon God as the final guarantor of human certitude. The result was that, for better or worse, our limitation by the Other in knowledge was discussed on the broader horizon of the essential finitude of human nature. In short, the epistemological dialectic of finite and nonfinite became involved in the theological dialectic of finite and Infinite. We have mentioned earlier that it is not easy to determine whether all the rationalist philosophers reduced the two dialectics to one; for some, indeed, a transcendent God became a deified Man. Nonetheless, the general framework of this discussion has persisted; the problem of God is still debated in terms of man's knowledge, and ultimately within the context of what man is. To that extent, we have not escaped the ambiguities of Kant's noumenon. Sartre's contribution to this debate, then, has grown out of his personal experience. From the idea that the otherness of God jeopardizes man's freedom and therefore man himself, he has further developed the suggestion of his experience that all otherness constitutes a menace.

It might be objected that this categorical statement is needlessly oversimplified and personally detrimental to Sartre. It cannot stand with his decision to ally himself with the F.L.N. in the late 1950s. It supposes, unmindful of its author's resilience, that the anthropology of *Being and*

Nothingness is still that of a free, disconnected consciousness that has no links through its body with the rest of
biological creation. Certainly the criticisms of Raymond
Aron, Maurice Merleau-Ponty, Pierre Naville, and Jacques
Houbart have played their part in correcting the vision, for
Sartre has been principally concerned with man as a being-
in-history, with one whose actions reflect the social and
economic realities of his milieu.

Without attempting here to complicate matters by
pursuing Sartre's later developments, we might note that
there is nothing in them to suggest that their creator has
revamped his basic "theological" orientation. Once man
has repressed the desire to be God, he is free to devote
himself wholeheartedly to the City of Man. The inherent
optimism of his spirit can be properly channeled if he can
be shaken out of an Icarus proclivity, a foolish attraction
forever to brush his wings against the consuming fires of
God and evil. This outlook is not simply the product of a
pathological obsession with evil, and theologians fail to do
it justice if they recommend our perusal of *The Devil and
the Good Lord* because it can force us to rethink God and
the devil in our daily lives, or make us see the necessity of
God if we are to escape the pitfall of the absurd.[11] Sartre, we
can plausibly argue, has quarried a monument out of his
personal experience. His childhood, as we know, offered
him no satisfying religious convictions, no genuine religious
encounter. Later, when he had become disgusted with sham,
his own above all, and met evil in some of its myriad shapes,
he rationalized a consistently atheistic position. It was life
as he met it that dictated this option. Perhaps the apathy of
Christians conspired with human perversity and sinfulness
to induce him to attack that otherness which theologians
have traditionally recognized as man's openness to religion.
In fealty to his own experience, Sartre could have not have

11. See Régis Jolivet, *Sartre ou la théologie de l'absurde* (Paris, Fayard,
1965).

argued atheism on the basis of "science," returning to the rationalist and empiricist premises which supported nineteenth-century French "radicalism." Nor could he have espoused that total immanence which Suzuki has described as the "sense of Zen":

> Salvation must be sought in the finite itself; there is nothing infinite apart from finite things; if you seek something transcendental, that will cut you off from this world of relativity, which is the same thing as the annihilation of yourself . . . Therefore the finite is the infinite, and *vice versa*. There are not two separate things, though we are compelled to conceive them so, intellectually.[12]

In passing, we might advert to this firm negation of the transcendent which, Suzuki says, distinguishes Zen from existentialism in spite of efforts to assimilate them. It accounts for the reluctance of many Western theologians to call Zen Buddhism a religion.

It is important to emphasize the anti-religious character of Sartre's experience. Founded on a freedom that is an opposition, a reaction against the Other, it is not the reductive experience—of the infinite to the finite, of eternity to time, of God to man—that we associate with a naturalist would ever pretend to be. Like Camus', his is a rupture that challenges the theologian on his chosen ground of dialectic—a unique sort of anti-theism insofar as it offers an interpretation of the breakthrough that constitutes experience as a revelation of a world denying God. Sartre, we might say, is an anti-theistic mystic in a way that no naturalist would ever pretend to be. Like Camus', his is a passionate disbelief.

We must be cautious here about terminology. The empiricist–rationalist tradition of philosophy has in the past been supremely contemptuous of mysticism. "Mystic," as it was for Hume, has rarely been anything but a term of opprobrium. Yet the tide is changing somewhat, not because our contemporary empiricists find a new clarity in the language of mysticism, but because it is more difficult today to sell a staple of their goods: that human reason is some kind of detached, objectively contemplating faculty. By referring to Sartre as a mystic, we are simply acknowledging that his analyses are meant to confirm an argument that has been commonplace since Hegel: that the abstractive functioning of the human mind creates by its movement of retreat or reflection an illusion of objectivity. Now, indeed, confirmation comes from every quarter, even from that of our most dispassionate sciences, that man knows only to the extent that he takes part in a world. If we are to experience something in chemistry or archaeology we must share their worlds of meaning. In such a plight we are all mystics—in the only sense in which the philosopher can professionally use this word—for the mystic, etymologically and essentially, is one who has been initiated and has thus become a communicant or participant. The esoteric element of mysticism, then, has nothing to do with mumbo-jumbo and secret oracles. Its language is perfectly intelligible to anyone who lives its commitment and is therefore testable by the shared experience it endeavors to articulate. Whatever, then, the profound differences that mark their thought, Sartre, Eliade, and Saint John of the Cross think in the common structure or pattern of mysticism.[13]

If Experience, the Real, the Absolute can ground different experiences or ways of articulating the world, what way is open to us for judging the truth of a particular commitment? Since Sartre's works are implicitly meditations upon this question, let us see what he offers as as a concrete, philosophical answer.

13. See Georges Morel, *Le Sens de l'existence selon S. Jean de la Croix* (3 vols. Paris, Aubier, 1960–61).

The portraits in depth of Genet and Baudelaire lay bare the features of men who have "lived their truth." Like the rest of us, they have been reflective and spontaneous, have acted intentionally and impulsively, have known in varying degrees the what's and why's of their daily decisions. Qua artist, Sartre has not only tried to interpret them for us (in a way that Genet felt to be an exhibition); above all he has argued in the concrete that truth is a valuation. Consciousness is verbally related to conscience because conscience is a committed consciousness. We must learn to take full responsibility for our chosen way of looking at things. This taking of responsibility, however, occurs only in a reflective consciousness which, because of its fearful consequences, many of us attempt to escape. Reflection makes us aware of our own tensions, just as it enables us to understand the anxieties that Genet felt but could not always identify. Besides, it compels us to respond, to choose our own way in opposition to the designs of others for us and to suffer the unavoidable doubts and uncertainties of self-justification. But why respond at all if a response, because it is reasoned, bears these troubling consequences? Because we must, Sartre maintained: negating consciousness is our prerogative and duty as men. He has interpreted this negation, however, as he did for Genet, in the light of childhood traumas. Consciousness is an option because Sartre had to choose deliberately to be himself; but it is his peculiar kind of negating because that is the view that has given unity to all of his experience. His option must be true, because in this totalization he has found his salvation.

Is not the religious moment par excellence that in which a subjectivity, ceasing to disperse itself indefinitely in everyday reality, regains its eternal being, becomes a calm totality in full possession of itself?[14]

14. *Saint Genet*, p. 63.

By a strange detour we are back upon familiar ground: that a true perspective on life is ultimately religious because it is self-integrating or personal.

The contemporary theist is keenly aware that he cannot convert a total outlook on life by logic, but at least he feels that this return to personalism offers him the opportunity to set forth on a common ground the rationale of his choice. Negatively, he tries to eliminate other humanistic options as destructive of the personal: the naturalist's as based on a scientific commitment that appears to be depersonalizing man and de-anthropomorphizing the world, and Sartre's as antithetic to personal relations (the Other). Sartrean man's absolute freedom cannot be Good News if in reality it is a substitution of egotism for personalism. Positively, he can point to Teilhard de Chardin's thrust toward cosmic personalization as manifestive of man's ineradicable need for the personal, and as proof that the total view of science does not have to be impersonal. Finally, if he is a Christian theologian, he will appeal to the religious history described in his Scriptures, since the initiating ruptures constituting experience are there described as theophanies, that is, as personal interventions. Abraham was called to leave his country; Moses was given a Name to authenticate his experience; all of the prophets, beginning with Samuel, received their vocations by personal invitation. Thus the Hebrews knew God through communion, for His presence among them was manifested by extraordinary hierophanies and other deeds worked on their behalf. When they refused to respond to Him, their chastisement was effected with fatherly love. They were reminded that He had brought them out of the bondage of Egypt, and their sin was described in the unmistakably personal terms of a lie, of an act of treachery, or adultery. In like manner, the sense of the Christian life is one of contact or union with Christ. Whereas in His mortal life Christ worked signs, that is, visibly manifested the presence of God in significant deeds, so now in his mystical life is He still present in His Church, the sign which enables Christians to experience Him through other signs or sacraments.

The gist of the theologian's argument is that life is satisfactorily lived and explained only in personal terms, as friendship, communion, or love. This is a constant of the history of religions. The Christian experience—for Kierkegaard was right: its language is that of commitment, of surrender to a person known and loved—is meaningless unless man is conceived in congruent terms. It cannot prevail, as Dryden has poetically reminded us, in a climate of rationalistic individualism:

> What weight of ancient witness can prevail
> If private reason hold the public scale?

It is, moreover, a holistic experience, not only in the sense that it derives its compelling intellectual force from the comprehensiveness of its vision (the totality of man's destiny), but also in the sense that an authentic openness of mind, a receptiveness to other opinions, has always been a requirement of its personalism. Is it too harsh to suppose that in the past some of the notable blunders of its intellectual apologetic stem from a failure to appreciate the need for this apologetic to be embedded in its fundamental precept: Love your neighbor as yourself. It is to be hoped that this important lesson will not be lost on today's ecumenical-minded theologians who are now called upon in an unprecedented way to measure themselves against non-Western and non-Christian experiences. What they make of these "revelations" will be carefully observed by all, both committed and noncommitted, since in no slight way will the balance of their appraisal witness for or against the truth of the Christian commitment.

NINE. RELIGION AND THE HUMAN CONDITION

> Behind the supernatural being of this order, as behind the supernatural beings of all orders, we thus find that there has in every case been a human personality.
>
> SPENCER, *Principles of Sociology*

It is premature to suggest that we have outgrown Spencer's reductionism, although as a theory of the origin of religion, his hypothesis about the cult or worship of the dead was in a measure already supplanted by E. B. Tylor before he had a chance to publish it in 1876. Yet this excerpt, ripped from its context in the *Principles*, embodies a basic truth that accounts for the perennial appeal of Feuerbach, Freud, and all forms of "rationalized religion." For religion, like thought itself, is eminently human. It is "rooted in anthropology" because as a revelatory structure it functions in a way congenial to the patterning of human intelligence, at whatever level this process may operate. Thus, by offering us the "pattern of patterns," a whole picture of the meaning of human life and destiny, it runs the risk of being characterized as just another form of knowledge, albeit of global pretensions, of which man is capable. It shares, too, in the mystery of the human condition, for we cannot investigate it in its native element of experience but only in the rites, gestures, and language that are the all-too-human manifestations of it. In the course of our reflections we have come to realize, perhaps, another distressingly human aspect of religious investigation. In moving forward within his environment, man takes with him, as Lévi-Strauss has shrewdly remarked,

> all the positions that he has occupied in the past, and all those that he will occupy in the future. He is everywhere at the same time, a crowd which, in the act of moving forward, yet recapitulates at every instant every step that it has ever taken in the past.[1]

As a consequence, we have been compelled to discuss religion in an historical perspective, in full awareness that the shape of our problems and of the language tools available for handling them has been hammered out on the anvil of a centuries-old human experience. However enticing another method might have appeared, we could not under any circumstances have broken the web for a simple gaze at the religious phenomenon. Nothing human is really uncomplicated. The apparently tangential issues that we have been forced to consider—truth, thought and imagery, language, culture—had to be seen as components of "the whole view," even though the unavoidable evolution of meaning within these concepts made the task of clear-cut definition impossible. The word "science," for instance, has frequently recurred throughout these pages. Hopefully, the reader has understood it within its varying contexts, since a once-and-for-all determination at the outset would evidently have been prejudicial.

At the beginning of our reflection, after pondering the subject of one's starting-point in thought, we came to the conclusion that questions are in reality questionings, interrogations stimulated by, conducted within, and intended for, a definite milieu. We cannot expect to escape the inevitable limitations of the human condition, however frustrating these may be to our universal claims. And so, when we talk about the matrix of experience, controlling values, and determining attitudes, we are in danger of

1. *Tristes Tropiques*, p. 396.

giving the false impression that these intellectual or
spiritual creations are utterly gratuitous. Presumably, it
makes no real difference how we see things, for the ideas
of proof and disproof are inapplicable to the broad picture;
only precise, restricted questions are susceptible of a
satisfactory, pragmatic test. Creativity, in other words, has
been equated with projection, so that it is purest chance if
an artist happen to communicate, that is, share "meaning"
or "truth" with any of us who are not privy to his conspiracy.

In our earlier chapters we were intent upon exposing
the suppositions and implications of this epistemology
principally because Hume's averment that to be a philosophical skeptic is "the first and most essential step towards
being a sound, believing Christian" is a preposterous
distortion of the human condition. Both the Cartesian
hermeneutic of Reason and the Humean observation of the
World are compelling because of their simplicity. They
bleach the world of surds and scrub the paradoxes out of
thought, so that something as complex (because close to
life) as the religious phenomenon disappears as an object
of intellectual challenge. God remained behind the scenes
as an assumption of the Cartesian mathematical, inductive–
deductive thought; he was intractable to Humean empirical
verification. Supposedly, then, man believes in a self-destruc-
tive sense that Tertullian could scarcely have intended—
quia absurdum ("ineptum"). This proposal hands religion
over to the "primitive," unreflective psyche, for no thinking
man could live at peace in such disharmony. The
unexamined life, as Plato testified, is not worth living.

In subsequent chapters we were concerned to discover
how religion, given the historical evidence that it is normal
or natural to man's condition, might be inserted into the
specifically human aspect of his conduct. A phenomenological investigation revealed thought to be a universalizing
process, an attempt to order reality into a comprehensible
whole. This holistic thrust is mirrored in language, for the

mystery of the word (literally, its sign-function), which becomes strikingly apparent in the anthropomorphisms of symbol and myth, lies in its power to express man as a being of "heaven and earth," simultaneously in continuity and discontinuity with material existence. Is not this ambivalence, so to speak, of the human condition epitomized in the struggle to be a person: to rise beyond the level of thing or object by transcending one's particularity in order to participate as a true individual in a society of persons? Man achieves himself, therefore, through a progressive deconditioning, through successive ruptures of material conditions in acts of reflection that carry him beyond the immediate into the realm of time and history, the proper demesne of spirit.

No one today can argue the achievements of modern science. But there are bona fide objections to Science as a theory of knowledge and man: one that emphasizes man's continuity with nature to such a degree that the discontinuity which forms religion's insertion point into the human condition vanishes. The Scholastics were not off the mark when they looked upon the rupture of reflection as the "obediential potency," the commencement of revelation and the starting-point of that different level of continuity known as "spiritual experience." The Kantian epistemology offers an apt illustration of a contrasting "metaphysics of finitude." Because its concentration on the human condition gives little play to deconditioning, it terminates in a noumenal–phenomenal dichotomy, a breach of knowledge and faith that shatters the holistic thrust of the human spirit. It is, accordingly, a philosophy that reflects and fosters a despiritualization which stands in direct opposition to the Yogic attempt to bind man together in order to do away with the dispersion and automatism of profane consciousness, to the "classic" Chinese tradition of a spontaneous self-mastery that accompanies one's incorporation into cosmic rhythms, to the shamanic mystique of the body's

ecstatic reliving of a spiritual experience that eludes
profaned man. For, from a religious point of view, the
real ambiguity of Kant's philosophy is that it incarnates
the deadlock between the religious and the secular. The
religious component of this thought is its focus on the
"form of inner sense," Time, as the ground for the operation
of the Transcendental Imagination. Thanks to this faculty
the Ideals of Reason, the unifying concepts which present
to thought its goal of a "primordial unity," have empirical
application. Here, indeed, is the bedrock of all spiritual
anamnesis. In opposition to this stands the here-and-now
secular: an empiricism that devaluates all transcendence for
the sake of the immediate and discrete sensible. From this
kind of world the real or whole man has been alienated. He
can find only objects, not his personal self.

The contemporary literature of philosophical theology,
particularly in English, cautions us not to be too sanguine
about discussing religion from a height beyond the
Humean-Kantian premises. On the other hand, even within
the compass of a reconciling dialectical thought—happily,
some theologians appear to be dropping their prejudices
against Hegel since they recognize that a dialectic more
aptly expresses the basic reconciling image of Christianity[2]
—the possibilities of both theistic and atheistic options
present themselves. Eliade, in a reflection on the sacredness
of the sky, has intimated how the question of value, and
therefore of freedom, undergirds the notion of experience
and its expression.

> All this derives from simply contemplating the sky; but
> it would be a great mistake to see it as a logical, ra-
> tional process. The transcendental quality of "height,"
> or the supra-terrestrial, the infinite, is revealed to man
> all at once, to his intellect as to his soul as a whole. The

2. See Samuel H. Miller's *The Dilemma of Modern Belief* (New York,
Harper & Row, 1963).

symbolism is an immediate notion of the whole consciousness, of the man, that is, who realizes himself as a man, who recognizes his place in the universe; these primeval realizations are bound up so organically with his life that the same symbolism determines both the activity of his subconscious and the noblest expressions of his spiritual life. It really is important, therefore, this realization that though the symbolism and religious values of the sky are not deduced logically from a calm and objective observation of the heavens, neither are they exclusively the product of mythical activity and non-rational religious experience. Let me repeat: even before any religious values have been set upon the sky it reveals its transcendence. The sky "symbolizes" transcendence, power, and changelessness simply by being there. It exists because it is high, infinite, immovable, powerful.[3]

The suggestion that the sky in its immediate being-there reveals itself *as* is an assertion of the intentionality of consciousness which manifests Eliade's Husserlian starting-point. Simply, we do not logically deduce a view of the sky from a rationally neutral sky-in-itself. Rather, we see it from the beginning *as* and thereafter proceed to draw our conclusions from this initial perspective. Our originating experience itself, therefore, can be religious or not, but it becomes a rational position or free commitment through the reflective process by which we further determine ourselves.

Sartre represented for us the articulation of an antireligious option. His childhood experience of otherness as an invasion led him, at least during his existentialist period, to repudiate all transcendence and to describe the dialectic of consciousness as a condemnation to freedom.

3. *Patterns in Comparative Religion*, Eng. trans. Rosemary Sheed (Cleveland, World, 1963), p. 39.

More recently, however, especially in the *Critique de la
raison dialectique* (at this writing we are anxiously awaiting
the direction of the completed work on Flaubert), Sartre
seems to have come to terms with the Marxist transcendence
to society. Like Lévi-Strauss, he now offers a less abrasive
alternative to Eliade's religious dialectic: one that requires
no rupture in the human condition other than that of
knowledge, no revelation beyond mere self-revelation.

Within the Marxist purview, which has always claimed
to be a rigorously scientific interpretation of events, this
choice is inevitable. As an anthropologist, Lévi-Strauss has
calculated with the tangible aspects of religion, items like
the ritual celebrations of the hunt and death which form
part of primitive man's effort to control the course of
nature. Since tribal life, especially in the harsh conditions
of a rudimentary, nomadic life, is dependent upon this
"control," the sociological functioning of religion seems
of paramount importance. In certain instances it appears
as the primary, if not the sole, ingredient of the cement that
holds a group or community life together. To the eyes of
the scientific investigator, a tissue of fabulous narratives
about heroic ancestors and of mythic accounts touching
their origins and settlement provides a people with the
rationale for their solidarity. Even life lived within the
shadow of dire necessity and at the "lower" levels of comprehension must have a meaning.

It is not derogatory to characterize the difference between
Eliade and Lévi-Strauss as one between an insider and an
outsider: the choice between these two options gradually
narrows down to the deeper levels of personal experience.
In a sense more profound than Spencer ever fathomed, the
religious man affirms "personality" behind supernatural
beings, and therefore demands that a "scientific" dialectic
of knowledge be complemented by a person-maturing
dialectic of love. Knowledge, we have noted, always operates
within a framework. It is a determining breakthrough, a

boundary-setting process whose limits, paradoxically, are forever receding but nonetheless horizon deploying. The dynamics of person, on the contrary, involves a recurring irruption. To be a person not only requires a continuous transcendence to the Other but implies for that reason an unsatisfied longing for fulfillment. Thus Eliade's symbolism of the sky suggests transcendence because we see high "up there" a horizon, the limiting Other of knowledge. Yet for us it is an expanding horizon, one that ever recedes before our gaze and therefore can also convey the impression of a boundless freedom of movement: a perpetual ascent, a constant going up and over that is the essence of infinite love. The Marxist dialectic, it would seem, does not exploit this restless dimension of man's spiritual dynamism. Only religion carries his spirit beyond the limits of time and history into the eternal and infinite and thus responds to man's instinct for total deconditioning.

The thread of argument in this book has been that the structures of the religious consciousness are those of the whole man, manifesting themselves by a forward reach for the totality of man and world in God. This comprehension is one of intellect or reason but not Pure Reason, balanced, that is, by the dynamics of love. Consequently, there will always be a problem of God, as well as of man, for reflective thought. Divine Revelation has its human grounding in man's self-revealing act of knowledge. But since both of these revelations, divine and human, function within a dialectic of commitment or love, there will invariably be room for a genuine philosophic choice. Human dialogue, even about the most serious and sacred topics, must of its essence be free.

BIBLIOGRAPHY

Only the principal works cited in the text, together with other sources that would be less familiar to the trained philosophical reader, have been included in this bibliography. Generally speaking, the readily available editions have been preferred.

Altizer, Thomas J. J., "Mircea Eliade and the Recovery of the Sacred," *The Christian Scholar, 45* (1962).

Anon., *L'Existence de Dieu,* Tournai, Casterman, 1961.

————, A Symposium on the Concept of God in the *Journal of Philosophy, 57* (1960), A résumé of papers for the 1960 American Philosophical Association (Eastern division) Meeting.

Ayer, A. J., and Copleston, Rev. Frederick, "Logical Positivism: Discussion between Professor Ayer and Father Copleston," in *Readings in Religious Philosophy,* Geddes MacGregor and J. Wesley Robb, eds., Boston, Houghton, Mifflin Co., 1962.

Balthasar, Hans Urs von, *Dieu et l'homme d'aujourd'hui,* French trans. Robert Givord, Bruges, Desclée de Brouwer, 1961.

Banton, Michael, ed., *Anthropological Approaches to the Study of Religion,* London, Tavistock Publications, 1966.

Barrett, William, ed., *Zen Buddhism: Selected Writings of D. T. Suzuki,* Garden City, New York, Doubleday, 1956.

Barth, Karl, *Gotteserkenntniss und Gottesdienst nach reformatorischen Lehre,* Basel, Zollikon, 1938.

————, *Fides Quaerens Intellectum: Anselms Beweis der Existenz Gottes in Zusammenhang seines theologischen Programms,* 2nd ed. Darmstadt, Wissenschaftliche Buchgesellschaft, 1958; *Anselm: Fides Quaerens Intellectum,* Eng. trans. Ian W. Robertson (Cleveland, Meridian, 1960).

Bartsch, Hans Werner, ed., *Kerygma and Myth: A Theological Debate,* by Rudolph Bultmann, Ernst Lohmeyer, Julius

Schniewind, Helmut Thielicke, and Austin Farrer, Eng. trans. Reginald H. Fuller, rev. ed. New York, Harper & Row, 1961.

Beck, L. J., *The Method of Descartes: A Study of the Regulae,* Oxford, at the Clarendon Press, 1952.

Berdyaev, Nicolas, *Christian Existentialism: A Berdyaev Anthology,* Selected and Translated by Donald A. Lowrie, New York, Harper & Row, 1965.

———, *The Destiny of Man,* Eng. trans. Natalie Duddington, New York, Harper & Row, 1960.

Berkeley, George, *The Works of George Berkeley, Bishop of Cloyne,* A. A. Luce and T. E. Jessop, eds., London, Nelson, 1948.

Bevan, Edwyn, *Symbolism and Belief,* London, Allen & Unwin, 1938.

Black, Max, *Models and Metaphors: Studies in Language and Philosophy,* Ithaca, N.Y., Cornell University Press, 1962.

Blondel, Maurice, *La Pensée,* Paris, Presses Universitaires de France, 1934.

Bochenski, Joseph, *The Logic of Religion,* New York, New York University Press, 1965.

Boekraad, Adrian J., and Tristram, Henry, *The Argument from Conscience to the Existence of God,* Louvain, Éditions Nauwelaerts, 1961.

Brandon, S. G. F., *Man and his Destiny in the Great Religions: An Historical and Comparative Study,* containing the Wilde Lectures in Natural and Comparative Religion delivered in the University of Oxford, 1954–57, Manchester University Press, 1962.

———, ed., *The Saviour God,* Comparative Studies in the Concept of Salvation Presented to Edwin Oliver James by Colleagues and Friends, Manchester University Press, 1963.

Brandt, Richard B., *The Philosophy of Schleiermacher: The Development of his Theory of Scientific and Religious Knowledge,* New York, Harper & Row, 1941.

Bruner, Jerome S., Goodnow, Jacqueline J., Austin, George A., *A Study of Thinking,* New York, Science Editions, Inc., 1962.

Brunner, Emil, *Revelation and Reason: The Christian Doctrine of Faith and Knowledge,* Eng. trans. Olive Wyon, Philadelphia, The Westminster Press, 1946.

Buber, Martin, *Eclipse of God: Studies in the Relation between Religion and Philosophy,* New York, Harper & Row, 1952.

————, *I and Thou,* 2nd ed., with a Postscript by the Author Added, Eng. trans. Ronald Gregor Smith, New York, Scribner's, 1958.

————, *Two Types of Faith,* Eng. trans. Norman P. Goldhawk, New York, Harper & Row, 1961.

Butler, Joseph, *The Analogy of Religion, Natural and Revealed,* New edition with Analytical Introductions and Explanatory Notes, New York, Bell & Daldy, 1868.

Camus, Albert, *Lettres à un ami allemand,* Paris, Gallimard, 1945.

Carr, Edward H., *What Is History?* New York, Knopf, 1963.

Cassirer, Ernst, *Language and Myth,* Eng. trans. Susanne K. Langer, New York, Harper & Bros., 1946.

————, *The Philosophy of Symbolic Forms,* Eng. trans. Ralph Manheim, 3 vols. New Haven, Yale University Press, 1953.

Chapelle, Albert, *Hegel et la religion,* Namur, Secrétariat des publications, 1964.

Cherry, Colin, *On Human Communication: A Review, A Survey, and A Criticism,* New York, Science Editions, Inc., 1961.

Chomsky, Noam, *Aspects of the Theory of Syntax,* Cambridge, Mass., M.I.T. Press, 1965.

Clark, Malcolm, "Logic and System: A Study of the Transition from 'Vorstellung' to Thought in the Philosophy of Hegel," doctoral dissertation, University of Louvain, 1960.

Conze, Edward, *Buddhism: Its Essence and Development,* with a preface by Arthur Waley, New York, Harper & Row, 1959.

Cox, Harvey, *The Secular City: Secularization and Urbanization in Theological Perspective.* New York, Macmillan, 1965.

Creel, H. C., *Confucius and the Chinese Way,* New York, Harper & Row, 1960.

Cruickshank, John, *Albert Camus and the Literature of Revolt,* New York, Oxford University Press, 1960.

Crystal, David, *Linguistics, Language and Religion,* London, Burns & Oates, 1965.

Dewart, Leslie, *The Future of Belief: Theism in a World Come of Age,* New York, Herder & Herder, 1966.

Dunne, C. S. C., John S., *The City of the Gods: A Study in Myth and Mortality,* New York, Macmillan, 1965.

Duméry, Henri, *Philosophie de la religion: Essai sur la signification du Christianisme,* 2 vols. Paris, Presses Universitaires de France, 1957.

———, *Le problème de Dieu en philosophie de la religion.* Bruges, Desclée de Brouwer, 1957.

Durand, Gilbert, *Les structures anthropologiques de l'imaginaire: Introduction à l'archétypologie générale,* 2nd ed. Paris, Presses Universitaires de France, 1963.

Earle, William, Edie, James M., Wild, John, *Christianity and Existentialism,* Evanston, Northwestern University Press, 1963.

Eliade, Mircea, *Cosmos and History: The Myth of the Eternal Return,* Eng. trans. Willard R. Trask, New York, Harper & Row, 1959.

———, "Le Créateur et son 'Ombre,'" *Eranos-Jahrbuch, 30* (Zürich, Rhein Verlag, 1962).

———, "Crisis and Renewal in History of Religions," *History of Religions, 5* (1965).

——— and Kitagawa, Joseph M., eds. *The History of Religions: Essays in Methodology,* Chicago, University of Chicago Press, 1959.

———, "The History of Religions in Retrospect: 1912–1962," *The Journal of Bible and Religion, 31* (1963).

———, *Images and Symbols: Studies in Religious Symbolism,* Eng. trans. Philip Mairet, New York, Sheed & Ward, 1961.

———, "Initiation et le monde moderne," in *Initiation,* C. J. Bleeker, ed., Leiden, Brill, 1965.

———, *Mephistopheles and the Androgyne: Studies in Religious Myth and Symbol,* Eng. trans. J. M. Cohen, New York, Sheed & Ward, 1965.

———, *Myths, Dreams and Mysteries: The Encounter between Contemporary Faiths and Archaic Realities,* Eng. trans. Philip Mairet, New York, Harper & Row, 1960.

————, *Myth and Reality,* Eng. trans. Willard R. Trask, New York, Harper & Row, 1963.

————, "Mythologies of Memory and Forgetting," *History of Religions, 2* (1963).

————, "Paradis et Utopie: Géographie mythique et eschatologie," *Eranos-Jahrbuch, 33* (Zürich, Rhein Verlag, 1964).

————, *Patterns in Comparative Religion,* Eng. trans. Rosemary Sheed, Cleveland, World, 1965.

————, "The Quest for the 'Origins' of Religion," *History of Religions, 4* (1964).

————, *The Sacred and the Profane: The Nature of Religion,* Eng. trans. Willard R. Trask, New York, Harper & Row, 1961.

————, *Shamanism: Archaic Techniques of Ecstasy,* Eng. trans. Willard R. Trask, Bollingen Series 76, New York, Pantheon Books, 1964.

————, "Structures and Changes in the History of Religion," *City Invincible: A Symposium on Urbanization and Cultural Development in the Ancient Near East,* Eng. trans. Kathryn K. Atwater, Chicago, University of Chicago Press, 1960.

————, "Survivals and Camouflages of Myths," Eng. trans. Willard R. Trask, *Diogenes, 41* (1963).

————, *Yoga: Immortality and Freedom,* Eng. trans. Willard R. Trask, Bollingen Series 56, New York, Pantheon Books, 1958.

Elkin, A. P., *The Australian Aborigines,* Garden City, N.Y., Doubleday, 1964.

Evans-Pritchard, E. E., *The Nuer: A Description of the Modes of Livelihood and Political Institutions of a Nilotic People,* Oxford, at the Clarendon Press, 1965.

Festugière, A. J., *Contemplation et vie contemplative selon Platon,* 2nd ed. Paris, Vrin, 1950.

Feigl, Herbert, and Scriven, Michael, eds., *Minnesota Studies in the Philosophy of Science, 1, 2* (Minneapolis, University of Minnesota Press, 1956, 1958).

Ferré, F., *Language, Logic and God,* New York, Harper & Row, 1962.

Feuerbach, Ludwig, *The Essence of Christianity,* Eng. trans.
George Eliot, New York, Harper & Row, 1957.

Flavell, J. H., *The Developmental Psychology of Jean Piaget,*
with a foreword by Jean Piaget, Princeton, Van Nostrand,
1963.

Flew, Antony, and MacIntyre, Alasdair, *New Essays in Philosophical Theology,* London, SCM Press, 1955.

Frankfort, Henri, *Ancient Egyptian Religion: An Interpretation,* New York, Columbia University Press, 1948.

———, *Kingship and the Gods: A Study of Ancient Near Eastern Religion as the Integration of Society and Nature,* Chicago, University of Chicago Press, 1948.

Freud, Sigmund, *Moses and Monotheism,* Eng. trans. K. Jones,
Garden City, N.Y., Doubleday Vintage Books, 1955.

———, *The Future of an Illusion,* Eng. trans. W. D. Robson-
Scott, Garden City, N.Y., Doubleday, 1957.

———, *Totem and Taboo,* Eng. trans. J. Strachey, New York,
Norton, 1952.

Garaudy, Roger, *From Anathema to Dialogue: A Marxist Challenge to the Christian Churches,* Eng. trans. Luke O'Neill,
New York, Herder & Herder, 1966.

Gadamer, Hans-Georg, *Wahrheit und Methode: Grundzüge
einer philosophischen Hermeneutik,* Tübingen: J. C. B. Mohr
(Paul Siebeck), 1960.

Gendlin, Eugene T., *Experiencing and the Creation of Meaning: A Philosophical and Psychological Approach to the Subjective,* Glencoe, Ill., The Free Press, 1962.

Glasse, John, "Barth on Feuerbach," *Harvard Theological Review,* 57 (1964).

Glockner, Hermann, *Der Begriff in Hegels Philosophie: Versuch einer logischen Einleitung in das metalogische Grund-
problem des Hegelianismus,* Tübingen, Mohr, 1924.

Grégoire, Franz, *Études hégéliennes: les points capitaux du
système,* Louvain, Nauwelaerts, 1958.

Gusdorf, Georges, *Mythe et métaphysique, Introduction à la
philosophie,* Paris, Flammarion, 1953.

Guthrie, W. K. C., *The Greeks and their Gods,* Boston, Beacon
Press, 1962.

Hallaire, Jacques, "Ils parleront des nouvelles langues," *Christus, 12* (1965).

Hamilton, William, *The New Essence of Christianity,* New York, Association Press, 1961.

Hanson, Norwood Russell, *Patterns of Discovery: An Inquiry into the Conceptual Foundations of Science,* Cambridge, at the University Press, 1961.

Häring, Theodor L., *Hegel, sein Wollen und sein Werk,* 2 vols. Leipzig, 1929, 1938 (reprinted by the Scientia Verlag, Aalen, 1963).

Harris, Errol E., *The Foundations of Metaphysics in Science,* New York, Humanities Press, 1965.

Hartshorne, Charles, *The Divine Relativity,* New Haven, Yale University Press, 1948.

——, *The Logic of Perfection and Other Essays in Neoclassical Metaphysics,* LaSalle, Ill., Open Court, 1962.

Hegel, G. W. F., *Lectures on the Philosophy of Religion, Together with a Work on the Proofs of the Existence of God,* Eng. trans. from the second German edition by E. G. Spiers and J. Burdon Sanderson, 3 vols. Routledge & Kegan Paul, 1895, New York, The Humanities Press, 1962.

Heisenberg, Werner, *Physics and Philosophy: The Revolution in Modern Science,* New York, Harper & Row, 1958.

Heller, Erich, *The Artist's Journey into the Interior and Other Essays,* New York, Random House, 1965.

——, *The Disinherited Mind,* New York, Meridian Books, 1959.

Hendel, Jr., Charles W., *Studies in the Philosophy of David Hume,* Princeton, Princeton University Press, 1925.

Hepburn, Ronald W., *Christianity and Paradox: Critical Studies in Twentieth-Century Theology,* London, Watts, 1958.

Herberg, Will, ed., *Four Existentialist Theologians,* A Reader from Works of Jacques Maritain, Nicholas Berdyaev, Martin Buber and Paul Tillich, Selected and with an Introduction and Biographical Notes by Will Herberg, Garden City, N.Y., Doubleday, 1958.

Hockett, Charles F., *A Course in Modern Linguistics,* New York, Macmillan, 1958.

Hocking, William Ernest, *The Meaning of God in Human Experience: A Philosophic Study of Religion,* New Haven, Yale University Press, 1912.

Holton, Gerald, ed., *Science and the Modern Mind: A Symposium,* Boston, Beacon Press, 1958.

Hook, Sidney, ed., *Philosophy and History: A Symposium,* New York, New York University Press, 1963.

————, *Religious Experience and Truth: A Symposium,* New York, New York University Press, 1961.

Hume, David A., *A Treatise of Human Nature,* reprinted from the original edition in three volumes and edited, with an analytical index, by L. A. Selby-Bigge, Oxford, at the Clarendon Press, 1955.

————, *Dialogues Concerning Natural Religion,* edited with Introduction by Henry D. Aiken, New York, Hafner Publishing Co., 1957.

————, *Enquiries Concerning the Human Understanding and Concerning the Principles of Morals,* reprinted from the posthumous edition of 1777 and edited with Introduction, Comparative Tables of Contents, and Analytical Index by L. A. Selby-Bigge, 2nd ed. Oxford, at the Clarendon Press, 1902.

James, William, *The Varieties of Religious Experience: A Study in Human Nature,* New York, Random House, 1902.

Jensen, Adolf, *Myth and Cult among Primitive Peoples,* Eng. trans. Marianna Tax Choldin and Wolfgang Weissleder, Chicago, University of Chicago Press, 1963.

Jolivet, Régis, *Sartre ou la theologie de l'absurde,* Paris, Fayard, 1965.

Jung, Carl, *Psyche and Symbol,* A Selection from the Writings of C. G. Jung, Violet S. de Laszlo, ed., Garden City, N.Y., Doubleday, 1958.

————, *Two Essays in Analytical Psychology,* Eng. trans. R. F. C. Hull, Cleveland, World, 1956.

Kant, Immanuel, *Critique of Pure Reason,* Eng. trans. Norman Kemp Smith, London, Macmillan, 1958.

Kaufmann, Walter, *From Shakespeare to Existentialism: Studies* in *Poetry, Religion and Philosophy,* Boston, Beacon Press, 1959.

———, *Hegel: Reinterpretation, Texts, Commentary,* New York, Doubleday, 1965.

Kazemier, B. H. and Vuysje, D., eds., *The Concept and the Role of the Model in Mathematics and Natural and Social Sciences,* Utrecht, Reidel, 1961.

Kierkegaard, Søren, *Concluding Unscientific Postscript,* Walter Lowrie, ed., London and New York, Oxford University Press, 1938.

Kneale, William and Martha, *The Development of Logic,* Oxford, at the Clarendon Press, 1962.

Knox, T. M., "Hegel in English-speaking Countries since 1919," in *Hegel-Studien, 1* (Bonn: H. Bouvier u. Co., 1961).

Koberle, A., "Vernunft und Offenbarung," *Zeitschrift für systematische Theologie, 15* (1938).

Kojève, Alexandre, *Introduction à la lecture de Hegel: leçons sur la Phénoménologie de l'Esprit,* 3rd ed. Paris, Gallimard, 1947.

Kroner, Richard, *Von Kant bis Hegel,* 2nd ed. Tübingen: J. C. B. Mohr, 1961 (two vols. in one).

Kuypers, Mary Shaw, *Studies in the Eighteenth-Century Background of Hume's Empiricism,* Minneapolis, University of Minnesota Press, 1930.

LaCroix, Jean, *Le Sens de l'athéisme moderne,* Tournai, Casterman, 1959.

Langer, Susanne K., *Philosophy in a New Key: A Study of the Symbolism of Reason, Rite, and Art,* Cambridge, Mass., Harvard University Press, 1951 (Mentor Books, 1959).

Lepp, Ignace, *Atheism in Our Time,* Eng. trans. Bernard Murchland, C.S.C., New York, Macmillan, 1963.

Lévi-Strauss, Claude, *Anthropologie structurale,* Paris, Plon, 1958.

———, *Mythologiques: Le cru et le cuit,* Paris, Plon, 1964.

———, *Totemism,* Eng. trans. Rodney Needham, Boston, Beacon Press, 1963.

———, *Tristes Tropiques,* Eng. trans. John Russell, New York, Atheneum, 1964.

Lienhardt, Godfrey, *Divinity and Experience: The Religion of the Dinka*, Oxford, at the Clarendon Press, 1961.

Locke, John, *An Essay Concerning Human Understanding*, A. C. Fraser, ed., Oxford, at the Clarendon Press, 1894.

Looff, Hans, "Der Symbolbegriff in der neueren Religionsphilosophie und Theologie," *Kantstudien, 69* (Köln, Kölner-Universitäts-Verlag, 1955).

Lowie, Robert H., *Primitive Religion*, New York, Grosset & Dunlap, 1952.

Löwith, Karl, *From Hegel to Nietzsche: The Revolution in Nineteenth-Century Thought*, Eng. trans. David E. Green, New York, Holt, Rinehart & Winston, 1964.

de Lubac, Henri, *Aspects of Buddhism*, Eng. trans. George Lamb, New York, Sheed & Ward, 1954.

————, *Le drame de l'humanisme athée*, 3rd rev. ed. Paris, Spes, 1945.

————, *La pensée religieuse de Teilhard de Chardin*, Paris, Aubier, 1962.

————, *Sur les chemins de Dieu*, Paris, Aubier, 1956.

Lukács, Georg, *Der junge Hegel: Über die Beziehungen von Dialektik und Ökonomie*, Zürich und Wien, 2nd ed. 1948 (1954 ed. Berlin, Aufbau Verlag).

Macmurray, John, *Persons in Relation*, the Gifford Lectures of 1954, London, Faber & Faber, 1957.

————, *The Self as Agent*, the Gifford Lectures for 1953, London, Faber & Faber, 1957.

Macquarrie, John, *Twentieth-Century Religious Thought: The Frontiers of Philosophy and Theology*, London, SCM Press, 1963.

Malraux, André, *The Temptation of the West*, Eng. trans. Robert Hollander, New York, Random House, 1961.

Marty, Martin E., and Peerman, Dean G., eds., *New Theology No. 2*, New York, The Macmillan Co., 1965.

Marcel, Gabriel, *Creative Fidelity*, Eng. trans. Robert Rosthal, New York, Farrar, Straus, 1964.

————, *Journal métaphysique*, Paris, Gallimard, 1935.

Maritain, Jacques, *The Dream of Descartes*, Eng. trans. M. L. Andison, New York, Philosophical Library, 1944.

Mascall, E. L., *The Secularisation of Christianity*, London, Darton, Longman & Todd, 1965.

Matthews, Gareth B., "Aquinas on Saying That God Doesn't Exist," *The Monist, 47* (1963).

———, "Theology and Natural Theology," *Journal of Philosophy, 61* (1964).

Merleau-Ponty, Maurice, *In Praise of Philosophy*, Eng. trans. John Wild and James Edie, Evanston, Northwestern University Press, 1963.

———, *Sens et non-sens*, Paris, Nagel, 1948.

Miller, Samuel H., *The Dilemma of Modern Belief*, New York, Harper & Row, 1963.

Mitchell, Basil, ed., *Faith and Logic, Oxford Essays in Philosophical Theology*, Boston, Beacon Press, 1957.

Mondin, S.X., Battista, *The Principle of Analogy in Protestant and Catholic Theology*, The Hague, Martinus Nijhoff, 1963.

Morel, Georges, *Le Sens de l'existence selon S. Jean de la Croix*, 3 vols. Paris, Aubier, 1961.

Mouroux, Jean, *L'Expérience chrétienne: Introduction à une théologie*. Paris, Aubier, 1952.

Munson, Thomas N., "Hegel as Philosopher of Religion," *The Journal of Religion, 46* (1966).

Murray, John Courtney, *The Problem of God: Yesterday and Today*, New Haven, Yale University Press, 1964.

Nagel, Ernest, *The Structure of Science: Problems in the Logic of Scientific Explanation*, New York, Harcourt, Brace & World, 1961.

Nakamura, Hajime, *The Ways of Thinking of Eastern Peoples*, Japanese National Commission for UNESCO, 1960.

Nédoncelle, Maurice, *Conscience et logos: horizons et méthodes d'une philosophie personnaliste*, Paris, Éditions de l'Épi, 1961.

Newman, John H., *An Essay in Aid of a Grammar of Assent*, New York, Longmans, Green & Co., 1888.

Nietzsche, Friedrich, *Gesammelte Werke* (Grossoktav Ausgabe), 2nd ed. Leipzig, Kroner, 1901–13. Readily accessible translations of *The Antichrist* and sections of *The Gay Science* in *The Portable Nietzsche*, selected and translated with an introduction, prefaces and notes by Walter Kaufmann, New York, The Viking Press, 1954.

Otto, Rudolf, *The Idea of the Holy*, Eng. trans. J. W. Harvey, 2nd ed. London and New York, Oxford University Press, 1952.

——, *Mysticism East and West: A Comparative Analysis of the Nature of Mysticism*, Eng. trans. Bertha L. Bracey and Richenda C. Payne, New York, Meridian Books, 1958.

Pears, D. F., ed., *The Nature of Metaphysics*, London, Macmillan, 1957.

Piaget, Jean, and Inhelder, Bärbel, *The Early Growth of Logic in the Child: Classification and Seriation*, Eng. trans. E. A. Lunzer and D. Papert, New York, Harper & Row, 1964.

——, *Introduction à l'epistémologie génétique*, 3 vols. Paris, Presses Universitaires de France, 1950.

——, *The Language and Thought of the Child*, Eng. trans. Marjorie Gabain, New York, Meridian Books, 1955.

Plantinga, Alvin, ed., *The Ontological Argument from St. Anselm to Contemporary Philosophers*, Garden City, N.Y., Doubleday, 1965.

Plotinus, *The Enneads*, Eng. trans. Stephen MacKenna, 3rd ed. revised by B. S. Page, with a Foreword by Professor E. R. Dodds and an Introduction by Professor Paul Henry, S.J., London, Faber & Faber, 1956.

Polanyi, Michael, *Personal Knowledge: Toward a Post-Critical Philosophy*, London, Routledge & Kegan Paul, 1958.

Rahner, Karl, "Wissenschaft als Konfession?" *Wort und Wahrheit, II* (1954).

Ramsey, Ian, *Models and Mystery*, London, Oxford University Press, 1964.

——, ed., *Prospect for Metaphysics: Essays of Metaphysical Exploration*, London, George Allen & Unwin, 1961.

——, *Religious Language: An Empirical Placing of Theological Phrases*, London, SCM Press, 1957.

Read, Herbert, *The Form of Things Unknown*, New York, Horizon Press, 1960.

Ricoeur, Paul, *History and Truth*, Eng. trans. Charles A. Kelbley, Evanston, Northwestern University Press, 1965.

Robinson, James M., and Cobb, Jr., John B., *New Frontiers in Theology: 1, The Later Heidegger and Theology; 2, The New Hermeneutic,* New York, Harper & Row, 1963, 1964.

Robinson, John A. T., *Honest to God,* Philadelphia, The Westminster Press, 1963.

Robinson, H. Wheeler, *Inspiration and Revelation in the Old Testament,* London, Oxford University Press, 1962.

Saporta, Sol., ed., *Psycholinguistics: A Book of Readings,* New York, Holt, Rinehart & Winston, 1961.

Sartre, Jean-Paul, *The Devil and the Good Lord and Two Other Plays,* New York, Knopf, 1962.

——, *Saint Genet, Actor and Martyr,* Eng. trans. Bernard Frechtman, New York, George Braziller, 1963.

——, *The Words,* Eng. trans. Bernard Frechtman, New York, George Braziller, 1964.

Scheffler, Israel, *The Anatomy of Inquiry: Philosophical Studies in the Theory of Science,* New York, Knopf, 1963.

Scheler, Max, *Vom Ewigen im Menschen,* Bern, Francke, 1954. Eng. trans. Bernard Noble, *On the Eternal in Man,* London, SCM Press, 1960.

Schleiermacher, Friedrich, *The Christian Faith,* Eng. trans. of the second German edition, R. H. MacIntosh and J. S. Stewart, 2 vols. New York, Harper & Row, 1963.

Schmidt, Erik, *Hegels Lehre von Gott: Eine kritische Darstellung,* Gütersloh, C. Bertelsmann, 1952.

Sebeok, Thomas A., ed., *Myth: A Symposium,* Bloomington, Indiana University Press, 1965.

Simmel, Georg, "Contribution to the Sociology of Religion," *American Journal of Sociology, 11* (1905).

——, *Lebensanschauung,* München, Duncker & Humblot, 1922.

Smith, John E., "Philosophy and Religion," *Thought, 39* (1964).

Söderblom, Nathan, *Natürliche Theologie und Religionsgeschichte,* Leipzig, Heinrichs, 1913.

Sterrett, J. MacBride, *Studies in Hegel's Philosophy of Religion,* New York, 1890.

Taylor, A. E., *The Faith of a Moralist,* Gifford Lectures of 1926–28, 2 vols. London, Macmillan, 1930.

Tennant, F. R., *Philosophical Theology*, 2 vols. Cambridge, at the University Press, 1928–30.

Tillich, Paul, *Biblical Religion and the Search for Ultimate Reality*, Chicago, University of Chicago Press, 1955.

Toulmin, Stephen, Hepburn, Ronald W., MacIntyre, Alasdair, *Metaphysical Beliefs: Three Essays*, London, SCM Press, 1957.

Ullmann, S., *Semantics: An Introduction to the Science of Meaning*, Oxford, Blackwell, 1962.

Urban, Wilbur Marshall, *Language and Reality: The Philosophy of Language and the Principles of Symbolism*, London, G. Allen & Unwin, 1939.

Van Buren, Paul, *The Secular Meaning of the Gospel*, New York, Macmillan, 1963.

Van der Leeuw, G., *Religion in Essence and Manifestation*, Eng. trans. J. E. Turner, with Appendices incorporating the additions of the second German edition of Hans H. Penner, 2 vols. New York, Harper & Row, 1963.

Vygotsky, Lev Semenovich, *Thought and Language*, Eng. trans. Eugene Hanfmann and Gertrude Vakar, Cambridge, Mass., M.I.T. Press, 1962.

Wach, Joachim, *Sociology of Religion*, Chicago, University of Chicago Press, 1957.

———, *Types of Religious Experience: Christian and Non-Christian*, Chicago, University of Chicago Press, 1951.

Walton, Robert C., *The Roots of Experience and its Interpretation by Science, History, and Religion*, London, SCM Press, 1965.

Werner, Heinz, *Comparative Psychology of Mental Develop-Exploration*, London, George Allen & Unwin, 1961.

Wittgenstein, Ludwig, *Philosophical Investigations*, Eng. trans. G. E. M. Anscombe, New York, Macmillan, 1957.

———, *Tractatus Logico-Philosophicus*, London, Routledge & Kegan Paul, 1958.

Zaehner, R. C., *Hinduism*, London, Oxford University Press, 1962.

———, *Mysticism Sacred and Profane: An Inquiry into Some Varieties of Preternatural Experience*, New York, Oxford, University Press, 1961.

INDEX

Index

45, 65, 75, 95; God and, 56, 119; determinism of, 81; biological and physical, 150

Naville, Pierre, 174

Negation, 45, 164–65, 167 ff., 177; in dialectic, 83–84, 97; of symbol, 95; problem of, 95; and time, 96; and transcendence, 103, 175; in man, 150

Newman, John, 22

Nietzsche, F., 5, 7, 23, 37, 45, 49–50, 58, 67, 75, 141, 146, 153, 172; *The Gay Science*, 141 n.

Nirvāna, 141, 147–48, 169

Observation, 54–55, 61, 182; Humean, 72; complexity of, 120

One, the, 17, 24, 27, 90, 107, 140

Ontological argument. *See* God

Oppenheimer, Robert, 62 n.

Otto, Rudolf, 67, 125

Parmenides, 18, 51

Paul (Saint), 15, 28

Pears, D. F., 60 n.

Peirce, Charles, 11

Pelagian, 1, 21

Person, 153–54, 165, 178, 180, 183, 186–87; world and, 25, 146 ff.; in religious "world," 48; God and, 50, 118; in experience, 96; self-achievement of, 112; in Buddhism, 146 ff.

Phenomenology, 6, 7, 75, 109, 136, 138, 154, 182; of religion, vii, 10, 134–35; of philosophy, 13; Hegelian, 14, 84, 100, 107; Husserlian, 84; Heideggerian, 88; of language, 112; and logic of religion, 113

Piaget, Jean, 20, 101, 131

Planète, 131

Plantinga, Alvin, 18 n.

Plato, 14–15, 19–20, 23–24, 42, 100, 104, 141, 182; *Republic*, 15 n., 23; *Meno*, 20

Plotinus, 17–18, 27–28, 90, 105, 106 n.; *Enneads*, 17

Popper, Karl, 76

Presupposition, 2, 3, 6, 11, 13, 118; of thought, 25, 121, 146; of truth and God, 37 ff.; Hume and Cartesian, 53 ff.; supposition and, 96 n., 120

Primitive(s), vii f., 47, 99, 134, 155, 182, 186; as origin, 123; thought, 129–130; and "center," 144

Proof, 182; and world of logic, 56; meaning of, 20, 25–26; absolute concept of, 72. *See also* God; Inference

Protagoras, 15

Protestant, 149; theologians, 4, 22; gift-salvation, 21; theology of man, 22

Proudhon, Pierre, 173

Pseudo-Denis, 21, 127

Rahner, Karl, 26 n.

Rāmānuja, 139

Ramsey, Ian, 127–28

Ranke, L., 70

Read, Herbert, 73 n.

Reality, ix, 52, 103, 153, 171; concept of, 19, 152, 159; systematized, 19; God or ultimate, 24, 140; Cartesian concept of, 41; and reason, 84–85; mythic vs. scientific, 102; symbol and, 133; divine character of, 143–44; as Nirvāna, 147

Reason, 93, 176, 179, 187; and faith, 1, 20 ff., 56 ff.; philosophy as natural, 1; constant of philosophy of religion, 4; operation of, 14; Kantian, 23, 98, 140, 184; natural, 30; Hegel and, 44; and God, 46; theologians and Cartesian, 48–49; and religion, 51; and senses, 58; flint notion of, 80; in Eliade and Sartre, 160; Cartesian, 182. *See also* Mind

Recollection, ix, 86, 91, 96, 99–100, 184